MW01602378

The Tower of London: The Haunted Past and Secrets of Royal Ghosts

Oliver Lancaster

Published by Oliver Lancaster, 2023.

While every precaution has been taken in the preparation of this book, the publisher assumes no responsibility for errors or omissions, or for damages resulting from the use of the information contained herein.

THE TOWER OF LONDON: THE HAUNTED PAST AND SECRETS OF ROYAL GHOSTS

First edition. July 15, 2023.

Copyright © 2023 Oliver Lancaster.

ISBN: 979-8223387794

Written by Oliver Lancaster.

Also by Oliver Lancaster

Chernobyl: Unveiling the tragedy. A Comprehensive Account of the Nuclear Disaster

The Bhopal Gas Tragedy: Unraveling the Catastrophe of 1984

The Deepwater Horizon Oil Spill of 2010: A Disaster Unveiled

Fukushima Fallout: Unveiling the Truth behind the 2011 Nuclear Disaster

Minamata Disease: Poisoned Waters and the Battle for Justice (1932-1968)

Evil Women: Unmasking History's Most Notorious Women

Bundy The Dark Chronicles: America's Infamous Serial Killer

Dahmer The Dark Chronicles: America's Infamous Milwaukee Cannibal

Zodiac The Dark Chronicles: America's Infamous Cryptic Killer

Bigfoot: The Comprehensive Investigation into the Elusive Legend

Chasing Legends: The Truth behind the Chupacabra

Chasing Legends: The Truth behind the Loch Ness Monster

Aokigahara Forest: The Heartbreaking Secrets of Japan's Suicide Forest

The Amityville House: The Haunting Secrets of America's Most Infamous Residence

The Tower of London: The Haunted Past and Secrets of Royal Ghosts
The Winchester Mystery House: The Riddle of Sarah Winchester's Mansion

Watch for more at https://tinyurl.com/olanc.

Sign up to my free newsletter to get updates on new releases, FREE teaser chapters to upcoming releases and FREE digital short stories.

Or visit https://tinyurl.com/olanc

I never spam and you can unsubscribe at any time.

OLIVER LANCASTER

Disclaimer

The information presented in this book is based on historical records, folklore, and accounts of paranormal experiences associated with the Tower of London. While efforts have been made to ensure accuracy, the author and publisher do not claim to verify the existence of ghosts or supernatural phenomena. Readers are advised to approach the subject matter with an open mind and acknowledge that individual perceptions and beliefs may vary. The book is intended for entertainment and educational purposes, and any experiences or interpretations are left to the reader's discretion.

The Tower of London: The Haunted Past and Secrets of Royal Ghosts

THE TOWER OF LONDON: THE HAUNTED PAST AND SECRETS OF ROYAL GHOSTS

OLIVER LANCASTER

Introduction

The Tower of London stands as a solemn sentinel amidst the bustling modern city of London, silently guarding centuries of history within its imposing walls. Steeped in mystique and surrounded by an air of intrigue, this formidable fortress has witnessed the rise and fall of kings, the pageantry of coronations, and the darkest moments of political intrigue. In this chapter, we embark on a journey through time to explore the rich history and enduring significance of the Tower of London.

The story of the Tower begins nearly a thousand years ago, in the wake of the Norman Conquest of England. It was William the Conqueror who initiated the construction of the White Tower, the fortress's central keep, around 1078. Initially intended as a symbol of royal power and a defensive stronghold, the Tower's complex gradually expanded over the centuries, acquiring additional towers, walls, and buildings, each contributing to its formidable presence.

Throughout its history, the Tower of London served as more than just a fortress; it was also a royal residence and a center of political power. Monarchs often utilized the Tower as a temporary dwelling or a safe retreat, taking advantage of its fortified walls and strategic location along the River Thames. The Tower became synonymous with royal authority, and its storied halls witnessed countless momentous events, including the birth of princes, the plotting of dynastic rivalries, and even the imprisonment and execution of kings and queens.

Perhaps the Tower's most infamous role was that of a prison. From its earliest days, the Tower housed a diverse array of captives, ranging from political opponents to high-ranking nobles. Notorious prisoners like Sir Walter Raleigh, Anne Boleyn, and Sir Thomas More were held within its grim confines. The Tower's subterranean chambers, known as the "Little Ease" and the "Salt Tower," bear witness to the agony and despair of those unjustly incarcerated.

The Tower of London has long been entrusted with safeguarding the Crown Jewels of the United Kingdom. The Jewel House, located within the fortress, has been their home since the 17th century. This precious collection of regalia includes the dazzling Imperial State Crown, the Scepter with the Cross, and the legendary Koh-i-Noor diamond, to name but a few. The Tower's role as the repository of these priceless treasures underscores its enduring significance as a symbol of royal authority.

Today, the Tower of London stands as one of the world's most visited tourist attractions, drawing millions of visitors each year. Its historical and cultural importance is recognized globally, as evidenced by its designation as a UNESCO World Heritage Site. Visitors flock to the Tower to witness the Changing of the Guard, explore the formidable battlements, and delve into the labyrinthine corridors that bear witness to centuries of intrigue.

THE TOWER OF LONDON: THE HAUNTED PAST AND SECRETS OF ROYAL GHOSTS

The Tower of London's history and significance are woven into the fabric of British heritage. It is a living testament to the triumphs and tribulations of the monarchy, an enduring symbol of power and authority, and a repository of royal treasures. From its origins as a medieval fortress to its modern-day status as an iconic tourist attraction, the Tower of London continues to captivate and enthrall all those who set foot within its ancient walls. In the following chapters, we shall delve deeper into the haunting past and unravel the secrets of the royal ghosts that linger within the Tower's hallowed grounds.

Beyond its historical significance, the Tower of London carries a reputation as one of the most haunted places in the world. For centuries, stories of spectral apparitions, eerie sounds, and unexplained phenomena have permeated its ancient walls. In this chapter, we delve into the haunting legends that surround the Tower, revealing the ghostly presence that lingers within its corridors and courtyards.

One of the most famous and frequently reported apparitions is that of the White Lady. According to legend, she is believed to be the ghost of Queen Anne Boleyn, the ill-fated wife of King Henry VIII. Anne Boleyn was executed within the Tower's confines in 1536, accused of treason and adultery. It is said that her tormented spirit wanders the Tower, clad in a white gown, her headless form forever searching for justice and redemption.

The tragic tale of the Princes in the Tower has captured the imaginations of many throughout history. In 1483, the young Edward V and his brother Richard, Duke of York, were imprisoned within the Tower by their own uncle, Richard III. They were never seen again, and their disappearance remains an unsolved mystery. It is believed that their spirits still haunt the Tower, their presence felt in the chilling whispers and ghostly apparitions reported by visitors and guards alike.

Even in death, the Tower's haunted history reaches beyond its walls. The ghostly figure of Thomas Becket, the Archbishop of Canterbury, is said to make spectral appearances near the Tower Hill area. Becket was brutally murdered in Canterbury Cathedral in 1170, but his spirit is rumored to have found its way to the Tower, where he appears in shimmering robes, clutching a cross, and emanating an aura of otherworldly serenity.

While the White Lady is often associated with Queen Anne Boleyn, another ghostly apparition linked to her is the Headless Specter. Witnesses have reported encountering a figure resembling Anne Boleyn, but with a chilling twist: her headless form cradling her severed head in her hands. This haunting manifestation is believed to represent the injustice and tragedy of her execution and serves as a haunting reminder of the Tower's dark past.

Lady Jane Grey, the ill-fated "Nine Days' Queen," is said to haunt the Tower with a spectral presence. Jane Grey was reluctantly placed on the throne in 1553 but was swiftly overthrown and imprisoned within the Tower. It is said that her ghost can be heard sobbing in the Beauchamp Tower and that her haunting cries echo through the night, coinciding with the chiming of the midnight bell.

THE TOWER OF LONDON: THE HAUNTED PAST AND SECRETS OF ROYAL GHOSTS

The Tower of London's reputation as a haunted place is deeply ingrained in its historical fabric. The tales of ghostly apparitions and supernatural phenomena add an additional layer of intrigue and mystery to this ancient fortress. The White Lady, the Princes in the Tower, Thomas Becket, the Headless Specter of Anne Boleyn, and the ghostly presence of Lady Jane Grey are just a few of the spectral inhabitants that contribute to the Tower's eerie reputation. As we continue our exploration, we will uncover more secrets and delve into the chilling encounters that visitors and guardians have experienced within these haunted walls.

THROUGHOUT HISTORY, tales of ghosts and spirits have captivated the human imagination, weaving themselves into the fabric of folklore and legend. Among these spectral beings, royal ghosts hold a particular fascination. These ethereal figures, believed to be the restless spirits of kings, queens, and other noble figures, evoke a sense of awe and intrigue. In this chapter, we embark on a journey into the realm of royal ghosts, exploring the beliefs, stories, and encounters that have shaped our understanding of these supernatural entities.

Royalty has long held a special place in human society, with kings and queens representing power, authority, and often divine right. As inheritors of the throne, they occupy a unique position in the collective consciousness, both in life and beyond. It is within this context that the concept of royal ghosts emerges, as the departed spirits of those who once wielded immense influence and ruled over nations.

The notion of royal ghosts is not confined to a single culture or era but is found in diverse societies across the globe. From ancient Egypt to medieval Europe, from Asia to the Americas, tales of regal spirits have permeated folklore and religious beliefs. These legends often reflect the cultural values, historical events, and religious or spiritual practices of the societies from which they originate.

Royal ghosts are often depicted as messengers from the beyond, carrying with them warnings, prophecies, or imparting wisdom to the living. They may be seen as guardians of their dynasties, watching over their successors or intervening in times of crisis. The appearance of a royal ghost is believed to hold great significance, and encounters with these otherworldly beings have been seen as divine interventions or harbingers of destiny.

The restless nature of royal ghosts is often attributed to the circumstances surrounding their lives and deaths. The weight of their responsibilities, the tumultuous nature of their reigns, or the manner in which they met their demise can contribute to the lingering presence of their spirits. Unresolved conflicts, tragic events, or untimely deaths may bind their souls to earthly realms, perpetuating their stories long after they have passed away.

Royal ghosts not only embody the individual figures they are believed to represent but also carry the weight of their dynastic legacies. Their presence serves as a reminder of past glories, the rise and fall of empires, and the enduring influence of royal bloodlines. They symbolize the ephemeral nature of power and the transcendence of earthly realms, bridging the gap between the mortal and the supernatural.

Countless tales of encounters with royal ghosts have been passed down through generations, recounted by witnesses who claim to have witnessed these spectral apparitions firsthand. These experiences vary from eerie sightings to auditory phenomena, with individuals reporting conversations, visions, or even physical contact with the otherworldly figures. While skeptics may dismiss these accounts as mere superstition or imagination, they contribute to the rich tapestry of royal ghost lore.

The concept of royal ghosts intertwines history, mythology, and the ethereal realm. These spectral beings, believed to be the remnants of once-mighty rulers, continue to capture our imagination, stirring our curiosity about the afterlife and the enduring influence of royalty. As we delve deeper into the stories and encounters surrounding royal ghosts, we will unravel the mysteries, legends, and secrets that surround these enigmatic entities, shedding light on their place within the realm of the supernatural.

OLIVER LANCASTER

Chapter 1: The Tower's Origins

———

The construction of the Tower of London was not a mere architectural endeavor but a reflection of the political, military, and symbolic aspirations of its time. In this chapter, we delve into the multifaceted reasons behind the Tower's construction, exploring its strategic significance, defensive capabilities, and the symbolic role it played in asserting royal authority.

One of the key factors that led to the construction of the Tower was its strategic location along the River Thames. Situated on the eastern fringes of the medieval City of London, the Tower commanded a crucial position, controlling access to the capital by water. Its proximity to the river facilitated trade, allowed for swift communication, and provided a vantage point for monitoring and protecting the city against potential invasions from the east.

The Tower of London was primarily conceived as a formidable fortress, designed to withstand assaults and secure the monarch's safety during times of conflict. Its robust defensive features, including its imposing walls, towers, and moat, made it a virtually impregnable stronghold. Moreover, the Tower served as a royal residence, offering a place of refuge and temporary dwelling for monarchs, ensuring their safety and projecting an image of power and authority.

The Tower's construction went beyond its utilitarian purposes, as it was intended to convey the absolute authority of the reigning monarch. Its impressive architecture and strategic position embodied the might and grandeur of the crown, serving as a physical manifestation of royal power. The Tower's existence symbolized the monarch's ability to protect the realm, maintain order, and exert control over the city and its subjects.

The Tower of London's imposing presence and reputation as an impregnable fortress played a crucial role in intimidating and deterring potential adversaries. Its formidable structure served as a stark warning to those who dared challenge the crown's authority. The sight of the Tower's menacing silhouette, along with its grisly history of imprisonments and executions, sent a clear message to would-be rebels and rivals, ensuring that obedience and loyalty to the crown prevailed.

Beyond its defensive and symbolic functions, the Tower also served as a repository for the crown's most valuable treasures and important documents. The Jewel House, located within the Tower's walls, housed the Crown Jewels, symbolizing the monarch's right to rule. Additionally, the Tower's archives safeguarded important state papers, legal documents, and royal charters, ensuring their protection and preserving the historical records of the realm.

The construction of the Tower of London was driven by a combination of strategic, defensive, and symbolic considerations. Its location along the River Thames provided a strategic advantage, while its defensive capabilities ensured the safety and refuge of the monarch. Symbolically, the Tower represented the might and authority of the crown, projecting an image of power and intimidation. Furthermore, it served as a repository for the crown's treasures and important documents. Together, these factors contributed to the Tower's enduring significance as a historical landmark and a testament to the ambitions and aspirations of the monarchy.

The Tower of London, a fortress of immense historical significance, was initially constructed with a specific purpose in mind. In this chapter, we explore the primary objectives that shaped the Tower's design and layout, shedding light on its original functions as a royal stronghold, residence, and center of governance.

At its core, the Tower of London was conceived as a royal stronghold, intended to serve as a formidable defense against potential threats and rebellions. Its strategic location on the eastern edge of the medieval City of London, combined with its robust architecture, made it an impregnable fortress. The Tower's layout was carefully planned to maximize its defensive capabilities, incorporating features such as thick stone walls, sturdy towers, and a deep moat.

The White Tower, the central keep of the Tower of London, stands as the most iconic and dominant structure within the fortress. Built by William the Conqueror in the late 11th century, it served as the core of the initial construction. The White Tower, constructed with white limestone, comprised multiple floors, including a basement, and housed chambers for residential, administrative, and ceremonial purposes. Its massive walls, up to 15 feet thick, ensured the safety of the royal occupants and housed provisions necessary for extended sieges.

Surrounding the White Tower, the Inner Ward encompassed a complex network of buildings that catered to the needs of the royal residents and administrators. The layout of the Inner Ward included structures such as the Great Hall, residences for the king and queen, chapels, and various administrative offices. These buildings served as the hub of the Tower's activities, providing spaces for governance, ceremonies, and domestic life within the fortress.

Beyond the Inner Ward, the Outer Ward extended, encompassing additional buildings and facilities that catered to the functional needs of the Tower. It included structures like the barracks for soldiers, storage facilities for weapons and provisions, stables, and workshops. The Outer Ward was designed to support the everyday operations of the fortress, facilitating its role as a center of military power and governance.

The Tower Wharf, situated along the River Thames, played a crucial role in facilitating communication, trade, and transportation to and from the Tower. It provided direct access to the river, enabling the delivery of supplies, prisoners, and guests, as well as serving as a departure point for military expeditions and royal processions. The Wharf also served as a symbolic gateway, with the Traitors' Gate serving as a chilling entrance for prisoners arriving by water.

THE TOWER OF LONDON: THE HAUNTED PAST AND SECRETS OF ROYAL GHOSTS

The initial purpose and layout of the Tower of London were rooted in the need for a royal stronghold and a center of governance. The fortress's design maximized its defensive capabilities, with the White Tower at its heart, commanding both respect and fear. The Inner Ward catered to the residential and administrative needs of the royal occupants, while the Outer Ward provided functional infrastructure for military operations and logistics. The Tower Wharf ensured river access and served as a symbolic entry point. Together, these elements formed a comprehensive and strategic layout, reflecting the multifaceted roles the Tower played in medieval society.

The Tower of London has been witness to a multitude of historical figures who left an indelible mark on its legacy. In this chapter, we explore the lives and stories of some early figures associated with the Tower, shedding light on their roles, triumphs, and tragedies within its formidable walls.

The Tower owes its existence to the vision and ambition of William the Conqueror, the first Norman King of England. After the Norman Conquest in 1066, William ordered the construction of the White Tower, the iconic centerpiece of the fortress. His reign saw the Tower evolve from a defensive structure into a royal residence and a symbol of Norman authority. William's decision to build the Tower laid the foundation for its future significance and set the stage for its rich history.

Thomas Becket, the Archbishop of Canterbury during the reign of King Henry II, found himself at odds with the king in a bitter dispute over the limits of royal power versus ecclesiastical authority. Becket sought refuge within the Tower on multiple occasions, using it as a safe haven during his clashes with Henry II. However, his time within the Tower was not to be his salvation. In 1170, Becket was brutally murdered in Canterbury Cathedral, his martyrdom solidifying his place in history and lending an ethereal presence to the Tower itself.

The tragic story of the Princes in the Tower remains one of the most enduring mysteries associated with the Tower of London. The young Edward V and his brother Richard, Duke of York, were sent to the Tower by their uncle Richard III, following their father's death. They were never seen again, and their fate remains uncertain to this day. The disappearance of the Princes in the Tower has fueled countless theories, haunting the Tower with a lingering sense of tragedy and sorrow.

Perhaps one of the most famous figures associated with the Tower is Anne Boleyn, the second wife of King Henry VIII. Anne Boleyn was imprisoned within the Tower's confines in 1536, accused of adultery and treason. She faced a trial and was subsequently executed within the Tower, marking a pivotal moment in English history. The ghostly presence of Anne Boleyn is believed to haunt the Tower, perpetuating the legend of her tragic end and leaving an imprint on its history.

Guy Fawkes, a figure synonymous with the Gunpowder Plot of 1605, has a connection to the Tower as well. Fawkes was apprehended while guarding barrels of gunpowder placed beneath the House of Lords, part of a failed plot to assassinate King James I and blow up Parliament. After his capture, Fawkes was taken to the Tower, where he faced interrogation, torture, and ultimately execution. His failed conspiracy is commemorated to this day on November 5th, with bonfires and fireworks lighting up the skies of England.

These early historical figures associated with the Tower of London played pivotal roles in shaping its narrative. From William the Conqueror, the Tower's founder, to the tragic figures like Thomas Becket, the Princes in the Tower, Anne Boleyn, and Guy Fawkes, each left an indelible mark on the Tower's history. Their lives, triumphs, and tragedies intertwined with the fortress, imbuing it with a sense of intrigue, significance, and haunted mystique that continues to captivate the imagination of visitors and historians alike.

OLIVER LANCASTER

Chapter 2: The Tower as a Royal Residence

———

Throughout its long and storied history, the Tower of London has been home to a number of notable monarchs. From temporary stays to extended periods of residence, these monarchs added a regal presence to the fortress and left an enduring impact on its legacy. In this chapter, we delve into the lives and experiences of some of the most significant monarchs who called the Tower of London their temporary abode.

One of the earliest monarchs associated with the Tower was Richard I, commonly known as Richard the Lionheart. During his reign in the late 12th century, Richard spent a considerable amount of time away from England, participating in the Crusades. However, upon his return, he was briefly imprisoned in the Tower by his political rival, Leopold V, Duke of Austria, who demanded a ransom for his release. Richard's captivity within the Tower serves as a testament to the political complexities of his era.

Edward II's relationship with the Tower of London was marked by both royal privilege and tragic downfall. As king, he resided in the Tower on several occasions, utilizing its secure confines as a place of refuge and residence. However, it was within the Tower that he met a grisly end in 1327. Imprisoned and deposed by his own wife, Isabella, and her lover, Roger

Mortimer, Edward II was allegedly murdered within the Tower, casting a dark shadow over his reign and leaving a chilling legacy within its walls.

Edward IV, one of the key figures in the Wars of the Roses, found himself residing within the Tower on two significant occasions. In 1460, during the conflict between the rival factions of Lancaster and York, Edward sought sanctuary within the Tower before ultimately emerging victorious and assuming the throne. Later, in 1470, Edward was briefly imprisoned within the Tower during the brief restoration of Henry VI. Edward's resilience and eventual triumph serve as a testament to the Tower's significance as a temporary haven and a strategic stronghold during times of political turmoil.

Elizabeth I, one of England's most iconic monarchs, resided in the Tower prior to her coronation in 1558. Elizabeth was imprisoned there by her half-sister, Queen Mary I, on suspicion of treason due to her Protestant beliefs. Despite the grim circumstances of her captivity, Elizabeth navigated the political dangers of her time and emerged as a resolute and transformative ruler. The Tower of London serves as a tangible reminder of her early struggles and eventual ascent to the throne.

The Tower of London played a prominent role in the turbulent reign of Charles I. During the English Civil War, Charles I was held captive within the Tower following his defeat by Parliament's forces. He was imprisoned for over a year before being brought to trial and ultimately executed outside the Banqueting House in Whitehall. Charles I's captivity and execution within the Tower marked a profound moment in British history, leading to the abolition of the monarchy and the establishment of the Commonwealth.

The Tower of London stands as a testament to the presence and experiences of notable monarchs throughout history. Richard the Lionheart, Edward II, Edward IV, Elizabeth I, and Charles I are just a few examples of monarchs who left their mark within its ancient walls. Their experiences within the Tower, whether one of temporary residence, captivity, or tragic downfall, serve as significant chapters in the rich tapestry of the Tower's history. Their stories continue to captivate our imaginations and remind us of the power, fragility, and resilience of those who wore the crown.

Within the fortified walls of the Tower of London, the royal inhabitants led lives that were unique, governed by regal protocols and the necessities of their positions. In this chapter, we delve into the daily routines and lifestyles of the monarchs who called the Tower their home, providing insight into their activities, rituals, and the challenges they faced within the confines of the fortress.

As the embodiment of royal authority, the monarch's daily life within the Tower revolved around ceremonial duties and public appearances. From the grandeur of state banquets to the solemnity of religious services, the monarch was expected to maintain a regal presence, entertaining important guests, receiving ambassadors, and participating in royal processions. These events served to reinforce the monarch's position and project an image of power and grandeur.

The Tower of London was not only a residence but also a center of governance. Monarchs often held council meetings within the fortress, consulting with advisors, discussing matters of state, and making important decisions that shaped the course of the realm. These meetings required careful deliberation and often involved the presence of influential nobles and government officials.

While the public face of the monarch was focused on ceremonial duties and governance, there were also private chambers within the Tower where the monarch could retreat and attend to personal matters. These chambers served as private living spaces, providing a degree of privacy and comfort. Here, the monarch could engage in personal correspondence, leisure activities, and spend time with family members and trusted confidants.

Religion played a significant role in the lives of the royal inhabitants of the Tower. Within the fortress, there were chapels and places of worship where daily religious observances took place. Monarchs often participated in religious services, attended masses, and conducted private prayers. The spiritual aspect of their lives offered solace, guidance, and a connection to the divine.

Even within the confines of the Tower, monarchs recognized the importance of physical activity and leisure pursuits. Hunting, archery, and falconry were popular pastimes among the royalty. The Tower's open spaces, such as Tower Green and Tower Wharf, provided opportunities for outdoor activities and recreation. These pursuits allowed monarchs to unwind, enjoy the company of courtiers, and momentarily escape the pressures of their roles.

Daily life within the Tower was not without its challenges. Monarchs lived with the constant awareness of potential threats to their safety and the stability of the realm. The Tower's formidable defenses and the presence of a loyal guard ensured the security of the monarchs. Vigilance, precautionary measures, and the use of skilled personnel were employed to mitigate the risks associated with their position.

The daily life and routines of the royal inhabitants within the Tower of London were a delicate balance between regal duties, governance, personal activities, and the challenges of security and protection. Ceremonial duties, council meetings, private chambers, religious observance, leisure pursuits, and security measures all played a part in shaping their daily existence. Within the walls of the fortress, the monarchs navigated the complexities of their roles, balancing the demands of power, the expectations of their subjects, and the human desire for privacy and leisure.

The Tower of London stands as a witness to a multitude of significant events that unfolded within its ancient walls. From political intrigue to executions, coronations to imprisonments, the fortress holds a rich tapestry of historical moments. In this chapter, we highlight some of the most significant events that have occurred within the Tower's storied confines, each leaving an indelible mark on its history.

The Tower of London has served as a site for numerous coronations and royal celebrations throughout history. One of the most notable coronations held within the Tower was that of William the Conqueror in 1066, marking the beginning of Norman rule in England. Other monarchs, including Richard III, Edward IV, and Edward V, were also crowned within the Tower's hallowed halls. These events symbolized the continuity of power and the affirmation of the monarchy's legitimacy.

The Tower's dark reputation as a prison is closely intertwined with its history. Many notable figures, including political opponents and members of the nobility, found themselves incarcerated within its walls. The imprisonment and subsequent execution of figures such as Sir Thomas More, Anne Boleyn, Lady Jane Grey, and Sir Walter Raleigh are among the most infamous episodes. These tragic events highlight the Tower's role as a place of punishment and the price paid by those who challenged the crown.

One of the most dramatic events associated with the Tower is the infamous Gunpowder Plot of 1605. The plot aimed to assassinate King James I and blow up the Houses of Parliament. Guy Fawkes and his co-conspirators were apprehended while guarding barrels of gunpowder beneath the House of Lords. Fawkes was taken to the Tower, where he faced interrogation, torture, and execution. The thwarting of the plot and the subsequent commemoration of Guy Fawkes Night on November 5th each year underscore the enduring significance of this event.

THE TOWER OF LONDON: THE HAUNTED PAST AND SECRETS OF ROYAL GHOSTS

The disappearance of the Princes in the Tower, Edward V and Richard, Duke of York, remains a haunting mystery. The young princes were imprisoned within the Tower by their uncle, Richard III, during the Wars of the Roses. Their fate remains unknown, and their disappearance casts a dark shadow over the fortress. This tragic episode continues to captivate historians and serves as a reminder of the Tower's grim history.

The Tower has also witnessed joyous occasions, such as royal births and marriages. Queen Elizabeth I, the daughter of Henry VIII and Anne Boleyn, was born within the Tower's walls in 1533. The marriage of Queen Mary I to Philip II of Spain was celebrated within the Tower in 1554. These moments of celebration and continuity showcased the Tower's role as a site of significant royal milestones.

In 1671, the Tower experienced a daring and audacious event known as the Jewel Heist. Colonel Thomas Blood, a notorious Irish adventurer, attempted to steal the Crown Jewels from the Tower. Blood managed to deceive the Jewel House keeper, but his theft was thwarted before he could escape. This audacious act and the subsequent capture of Blood added another layer of intrigue to the Tower's history.

The Tower of London's walls have borne witness to a multitude of significant events that have shaped the course of history. Coronations, imprisonments, executions, plots, births, and thefts have all left their mark on the fortress's legacy. These events reflect the complex tapestry of human triumphs, tragedies, and political intrigue that unfolded within the

Tower's formidable walls, cementing its enduring significance as a site of historical importance.

THE TOWER OF LONDON: THE HAUNTED PAST AND SECRETS OF ROYAL GHOSTS

Chapter 3: Anne Boleyn's Ghost

———

Anne Boleyn, one of the most fascinating and enigmatic figures in English history, captivated the attention of King Henry VIII and the nation alike. Her life, marriage to Henry VIII, and subsequent execution remain subjects of intense historical interest. In this chapter, we delve into the story of Anne Boleyn, examining her early life, rise to power, tumultuous marriage, and tragic downfall.

Anne Boleyn was born around the year 1501, the daughter of Sir Thomas Boleyn and Lady Elizabeth Howard. She received a Renaissance education, which included learning languages, music, literature, and the arts. Anne spent a significant portion of her youth in the court of the Netherlands, where she gained exposure to continental ideas and culture, shaping her outlook and demeanor.

Anne's return to England marked the beginning of her ascent in courtly circles. She initially served as a lady-in-waiting to Queen Catherine of Aragon, Henry VIII's first wife. Anne's wit, intelligence, and charm captured the attention of the king, and their relationship evolved into a romantic affair. Anne's refusal to become Henry VIII's mistress and insistence on marriage placed immense pressure on the king, leading to the annulment of his marriage to Catherine and the subsequent break with the Catholic Church.

Anne Boleyn became Queen Consort of England after her marriage to Henry VIII in 1533. As queen, Anne wielded significant influence, promoting religious reform and encouraging the growth of Protestant ideas. She played a pivotal role in fostering the English Reformation, supporting scholars and theologians who challenged Catholic doctrine and sought to establish a more independent English church.

However, Anne's position as queen was fraught with challenges and controversies. Her inability to produce a male heir, combined with the growing dissatisfaction of the nobility and the populace, eroded her support at court. Anne's sharp wit and outspoken nature made her enemies, and accusations of adultery, incest, and treason began to circulate. The arrest and trial of several members of her inner circle, including her brother George Boleyn, heightened the tensions and set the stage for her tragic downfall.

In 1536, Anne Boleyn was arrested and charged with adultery, treason, and plotting against the king's life. After a highly controversial trial, in which she was found guilty, Anne was sentenced to death. On May 19, 1536, she was executed within the Tower of London. Her death was swift and carried out by the skilled French swordsman, providing her with a measure of mercy compared to the more common methods of execution at the time.

Anne Boleyn's life and tragic end left an indelible mark on history. Her marriage to Henry VIII was a turning point in English history, leading to the break from Rome and the establishment of the Church of England. Her influence as queen and patron of the arts left a cultural legacy, and her story has fascinated writers, artists, and historians for centuries. Anne's execution was a pivotal moment, marking the end of a tumultuous era and heralding the changes that would shape England's religious and political landscape.

Anne Boleyn's life journey from a young courtier to queen consort, her profound impact on religious reform, and her ultimate downfall and execution within the Tower of London are captivating chapters in history. Her story is one of ambition, political maneuvering, love, and tragedy. Anne's legacy endures, offering a glimpse into the complex dynamics of power, gender, and religion during the turbulent reign of Henry VIII.

The haunting presence of Anne Boleyn is said to linger within the Tower of London long after her tragic execution. Reports of spectral sightings, eerie phenomena, and unexplained occurrences have given rise to a wealth of legends surrounding her ghost. In this chapter, we explore the reports and legends that surround the ghostly presence of Anne Boleyn, delving into the chilling encounters and the enduring fascination with her ethereal manifestation.

Over the centuries, numerous witnesses have reported encountering the ghostly figure of Anne Boleyn within the Tower's walls. She is often described as a lady dressed in a white gown, her presence accompanied by a sense of melancholy and an air of tragedy. Visitors, guards, and even members of the royal family have claimed to witness her spectral form walking the corridors, gazing out of windows, or appearing near the site of her execution.

One of the most haunting legends associated with Anne Boleyn's ghost is that of her headless apparition. Some witnesses claim to have encountered a spectral figure resembling Anne Boleyn, but with a chilling twist: her headless form cradling her severed head in her hands. This macabre manifestation is believed to symbolize the injustice and tragedy of her execution and serves as a haunting reminder of her tumultuous fate.

Reports of eerie sounds and inexplicable sensations often accompany encounters with Anne Boleyn's ghost. Visitors have reported hearing footsteps echoing through empty corridors, whispers carried by the wind, and the rustling of a long gown. Some witnesses claim to feel a sudden drop in temperature, an overwhelming sense of sadness, or a feeling of being watched in certain areas associated with Anne Boleyn's presence. These experiences add to the eerie atmosphere and the authenticity of the ghostly tales.

There have been accounts of individuals claiming to have had direct interactions with Anne Boleyn's ghost. Some witnesses assert that they engaged in conversations with her, experiencing her as a fully formed apparition capable of communicating with the living. These encounters often evoke a sense of compassion and sadness, with Anne Boleyn expressing her longing for justice or conveying messages from beyond the grave.

THE TOWER OF LONDON: THE HAUNTED PAST AND SECRETS OF ROYAL GHOSTS

The legends surrounding Anne Boleyn's ghost have permeated popular culture, literature, and the arts. From novels to films and stage productions, her spectral presence has continued to captivate audiences and fuel the imagination. The enduring fascination with her ghost reflects the ongoing interest in Anne Boleyn's life, her tragic fate, and the enduring mysteries that surround her legacy.

While many firmly believe in the existence of Anne Boleyn's ghost, skepticism persists. Some argue that the reports and legends are a product of historical imagination, influenced by the Tower's reputation and the desire to perpetuate the haunting atmosphere. Skeptics attribute the sightings and experiences to suggestibility, psychological factors, or even intentional fabrication. However, the weight of the accounts and the consistency of the stories add a compelling dimension to the tales of Anne Boleyn's ghost.

The reports and legends surrounding Anne Boleyn's ghost within the Tower of London continue to captivate believers, skeptics, and historians alike. Sightings, sounds, and sensations experienced by witnesses have fueled the enduring fascination with her spectral presence. Whether a figment of imagination or an actual ethereal manifestation, the ghostly aura surrounding Anne Boleyn adds to the mystique of the Tower, perpetuating her tragic story and keeping her memory alive within its ancient walls.

The ghostly presence of Anne Boleyn within the Tower of London has been the subject of numerous accounts, each adding to the chilling lore surrounding her tragic fate. In this chapter, we delve into specific sightings and experiences attributed to the ghost of Anne Boleyn, recounting the eerie encounters and the vivid descriptions given by those who claim to have encountered her spectral form.

One of the most commonly reported sightings of Anne Boleyn's ghost is within the corridors of the Tower. Witnesses have described encountering a lady dressed in a white gown, matching the historical depiction of Anne Boleyn. The apparition is said to glide silently, her presence evoking a sense of melancholy and a deep feeling of sorrow. Witnesses have reported catching fleeting glimpses of her figure before she fades away, leaving behind a lingering feeling of her ethereal presence.

The Chapel Royal of St. Peter ad Vincula within the Tower is said to be a significant site of Anne Boleyn's ghostly activity. Several visitors and members of the clergy have claimed to witness her ghost kneeling in prayer or walking silently through the pews. Some have reported hearing soft whispers or sobs coming from the area where Anne's remains are interred. The chapel's atmosphere becomes charged with a sense of tragedy and an eerie stillness when her ghost is said to be present.

One particular sighting associated with Anne Boleyn's ghost is centered around the window of the White Tower, the iconic keep of the fortress. Witnesses have reported seeing a figure resembling Anne Boleyn looking out from the window, her ghostly presence captivating and haunting. The image of her spectral form gazing out over the Tower grounds evokes a profound sense of melancholy and reflection, as if she is forever trapped within her tragic fate.

A particularly chilling manifestation attributed to Anne Boleyn's ghost is that of her headless form. Several witnesses claim to have encountered a spectral figure resembling Anne Boleyn, but with her head conspicuously absent. These encounters often occur near the site of her execution, evoking a vivid and unsettling image of her holding her severed head in her hands. This harrowing sight serves as a chilling reminder of the violent end she met and the injustice she suffered.

In addition to sightings, there have been accounts of individuals claiming to have interacted with Anne Boleyn's ghost. Some witnesses assert having engaged in conversations with her, experiencing her as a fully formed apparition capable of communicating with the living. These interactions have been described as brief but poignant, with Anne expressing her longing for justice or conveying messages of forgiveness and redemption.

The specific sightings and experiences attributed to Anne Boleyn's ghost within the Tower of London paint a vivid picture of her ethereal presence. From the corridors to the chapel, the window to the site of her execution, witnesses have reported encountering a spectral figure matching the historical depiction of Anne Boleyn. These encounters evoke a sense of melancholy, sorrow, and tragedy, contributing to the enduring fascination with her ghostly apparition. Whether believed as genuine encounters or dismissed as products of imagination, the tales of Anne Boleyn's ghost continue to captivate and send shivers down the spines of those who visit the Tower.

THE TOWER OF LONDON: THE HAUNTED PAST AND SECRETS OF ROYAL GHOSTS

Chapter 4: The White Tower

The Tower of London stands as a remarkable testament to medieval architecture and engineering. Its construction, layout, and purpose were meticulously designed to serve as a stronghold, a royal residence, and a symbol of authority. In this chapter, we explore the fascinating details of the Tower's construction, its architectural features, and the multifaceted purposes it served throughout history.

The construction of the Tower of London began in the late 11th century under the orders of William the Conqueror. The primary focus was the central keep known as the White Tower, which served as the nucleus of the fortress. Built with Caen stone imported from Normandy, the White Tower showcased a combination of Romanesque and Norman architectural styles. Over the centuries, additional structures and fortifications were added, expanding the Tower's size and defensive capabilities.

The White Tower, the most prominent structure within the fortress, stands as an iconic example of Norman architecture. It is characterized by its massive square shape, towering walls, and corner turrets. The walls of the White Tower are constructed using layers of stone, with the lower sections being thicker and more robust. Inside the tower, spiral staircases, chambers, and halls provided living spaces for the royal inhabitants, while arrow loops and embrasures offered defensive positions.

The Tower's walls, encircling the Inner Ward and the Outer Ward, were constructed with layers of stone and flint, creating a formidable defensive barrier. Circular towers, such as the Bell Tower and the Beauchamp Tower, punctuated the walls, providing lookout points and additional living spaces. A moat, originally filled by the waters of the River Thames, enhanced the fortress's defenses.

The Tower of London served a multitude of purposes throughout its history. Initially built as a royal stronghold, its primary function was to protect the monarch, the city, and the realm from external threats. The Tower's location on the eastern fringes of the medieval City of London allowed for control of river traffic and facilitated the defense of the capital.

As a royal residence, the Tower provided temporary accommodations for monarchs and their retinues. The Inner Ward housed residences, such as the Royal Apartments and the Queen's House, where the royal family could live comfortably within the fortress's secure confines. The presence of a chapel, such as the Chapel Royal of St. Peter ad Vincula, ensured the spiritual needs of the residents were met.

The Tower of London also served as a center of governance. Council meetings, court hearings, and other administrative functions took place within the Tower, making it a hub of political activity. The Tower's infamous dungeons, including the Bloody Tower and the Wakefield Tower, were used to house prisoners of high rank, serving as a visible symbol of royal authority and control.

THE TOWER OF LONDON: THE HAUNTED PAST AND SECRETS OF ROYAL GHOSTS

Beyond its practical functions, the Tower of London carried great symbolic significance. Its imposing architecture, robust defenses, and strategic location made it an emblem of royal power, projecting authority and strength. The Crown Jewels, housed within the Jewel House, symbolized the monarch's right to rule and were displayed to reinforce the Tower's regal associations. Ceremonies, such as coronations and public processions, further enhanced the Tower's symbolism and cemented its place in the collective imagination of the nation.

The construction, architecture, and purpose of the Tower of London are intertwined in a complex tapestry of medieval engineering, regal aspirations, and strategic considerations. The White Tower, with its imposing presence and distinctive features, stands as the centerpiece of the fortress, representing the culmination of Norman and Romanesque design. From its role as a stronghold to its function as a royal residence and center of governance, the Tower of London has left an indelible mark on history, serving as a tangible reminder of the ambitions, power, and symbolism associated with the English monarchy.

The White Tower, the central keep of the Tower of London, has witnessed numerous significant historical events throughout its existence. From royal ceremonies to political intrigue, battles to imprisonments, the White Tower stands as a silent witness to the unfolding of history. In this chapter, we highlight some of the most notable events associated with the White Tower, each leaving an indelible mark on its storied past.

The construction of the White Tower itself marked a significant event in English history. Ordered by William the Conqueror in the late 11th century, its construction symbolized the establishment of Norman rule in England. The completion of the White Tower showcased the architectural prowess of the Normans and solidified their authority over the conquered land.

The White Tower has been the site of several coronations and royal ceremonies, adding a regal touch to its history. In 1189, Richard I (Richard the Lionheart) was crowned within its walls, marking the beginning of his reign. The Tower also witnessed the coronations of monarchs such as Edward IV, Henry VI, and Henry VIII. These ceremonies held within the White Tower reinforced the legitimacy of the monarchy and celebrated the continuity of power.

The White Tower has served as a place of imprisonment and execution for prominent figures throughout history. In the 13th century, the Tower witnessed the imprisonment and subsequent death of Simon de Montfort, a key figure in the conflict between King Henry III and the barons. The Duke of Clarence, George Plantagenet, was executed within the White Tower in 1478. These events exemplify the Tower's role as a place of punishment and the exercise of royal authority.

The White Tower has long been the home of the Crown Jewels of England. Since the reign of Henry III, the Jewel House within the White Tower has safeguarded the regalia, including crowns, scepters, and orbs, which symbolize the monarchy's power and authority. The presence of the Crown Jewels in the White Tower adds to its aura as a repository of national treasures and regal splendor.

The White Tower has been a site of scientific observations and experiments throughout history. In the 17th century, King Charles II established a Royal Observatory within the tower, which served as a center for astronomical research and the measurement of time. Astronomers such as John Flamsteed and Edmond Halley made significant contributions to the field from within the White Tower, enhancing our understanding of the universe.

The White Tower has not been immune to disasters. In 1841, a devastating fire engulfed the upper floors of the keep, resulting in substantial damage to its interior. The subsequent restoration, led by architect Anthony Salvin, sought to preserve the historical integrity of the White Tower while making necessary repairs and renovations. The fire and subsequent restoration efforts stand as important events in the White Tower's history, highlighting the challenges faced in its preservation.

The White Tower's history is intertwined with numerous significant events that have shaped the course of English history. From its construction as a symbol of Norman rule to its role in coronations, imprisonments, and scientific experiments, the White Tower has played a pivotal role in the nation's story. Its connection to the Crown Jewels, the ravages of fire, and subsequent restoration further enhance its historical significance. As the focal point of the Tower of London, the

White Tower stands as a living testament to the triumphs, tragedies, and enduring legacy of the English monarchy.

The White Tower, the iconic central keep of the Tower of London, is not only known for its historical significance but also for the ghostly phenomena reported within its ancient walls. Over the centuries, visitors, guards, and even members of the royal family have claimed to witness eerie occurrences and spectral apparitions. In this chapter, we explore the ghostly phenomena reported within the White Tower, delving into chilling encounters and the enduring mystery that surrounds its paranormal reputation.

One of the most haunting tales associated with the White Tower is the presence of the ghostly apparitions of the Princes in the Tower, Edward V and Richard, Duke of York. According to legend, their spirits wander the tower in search of rest and justice. Witnesses have reported seeing the ghostly figures of young boys wearing clothing from the medieval period, their presence evoking a sense of sorrow and tragedy. The ethereal manifestations of the Princes in the Tower add to the enduring mystique and chilling reputation of the White Tower.

Another frequently reported ghostly phenomenon within the White Tower is the apparition of a figure in armor. Witnesses describe encountering a spectral presence dressed in ancient armor, wielding a sword or a spear. The ghostly figure often appears near the armory or the White Tower's walls, exuding an aura of authority and military prowess. Some speculate that this spectral manifestation could be linked to the many warriors and historical figures associated with the Tower's past.

THE TOWER OF LONDON: THE HAUNTED PAST AND SECRETS OF ROYAL GHOSTS

As one of the most famous historical figures associated with the Tower, it is no surprise that Anne Boleyn's ghost is said to haunt the White Tower. Witnesses have reported encountering a spectral lady dressed in Tudor-era clothing, believed to be the ghost of Anne Boleyn. She is often described as wearing a white gown, with a melancholic expression and a sense of sadness surrounding her presence. Sightings of Anne Boleyn's ghost within the White Tower add a chilling layer to the haunting legacy of this iconic structure.

In addition to visual apparitions, there have been reports of eerie sounds and unexplained sensations within the White Tower. Visitors and guards have claimed to hear footsteps echoing through empty corridors, doors creaking, and whispers carried on the air. Some have reported sudden drops in temperature or an overwhelming feeling of unease, as if they were being watched or accompanied by an unseen presence. These unexplained phenomena contribute to the atmospheric and otherworldly ambiance within the White Tower.

Poltergeist activity, characterized by objects moving inexplicably or sudden disturbances, has also been reported within the White Tower. Guards have described objects being thrown or displaced without any apparent cause. Some accounts speak of furniture rearranging itself or doors slamming shut on their own. These manifestations of poltergeist activity add an element of unpredictability and unease to the ghostly phenomena associated with the White Tower.

The White Tower, with its rich history and architectural grandeur, is also a place where ghostly phenomena have been reported for centuries. The apparitions of the Princes in the Tower, the spectral figure in armor, and the ghost of Anne Boleyn are among the most frequently encountered paranormal entities within its walls. Eerie sounds, unexplained sensations, and poltergeist activity further contribute to the haunted reputation of the White Tower. Whether these encounters are attributed to overactive imaginations, historical echoes, or genuine paranormal phenomena, they add to the mystique and fascination surrounding this iconic structure, making it a magnet for those intrigued by the supernatural.

THE TOWER OF LONDON: THE HAUNTED PAST AND SECRETS OF ROYAL GHOSTS

Chapter 5: The Bloody Tower

———

The name "White Tower" carries with it an air of mystique and evokes images of grandeur and power. However, behind this seemingly innocuous name lies a history intertwined with bloodshed, violence, and power struggles. In this chapter, we explore the origins of the White Tower's name and the events that led to its association with bloodshed, solidifying its reputation as a symbol of authority and brutality.

The White Tower derives its name from the distinctive white hue of its stone exterior. Constructed using Caen stone imported from Normandy, the tower's walls were designed to be visually striking and formidable. The use of white stone was not only an aesthetic choice but also a symbol of prestige and opulence. The name "White Tower" became associated with the central keep, and over time, it became synonymous with the entire fortress.

The White Tower's association with bloodshed stems from its historical role as a fortress, prison, and site of executions. The Tower of London, including the White Tower, became a symbol of royal authority and control, where acts of violence and power were carried out in the name of the monarchy.

The Tower witnessed numerous executions, and its infamous Traitor's Gate played a significant role in these bloody events. Traitor's Gate served as the entrance for prisoners brought by boat to the Tower, often destined for imprisonment and execution. Prominent figures such as Anne Boleyn, Sir Thomas More, and Lady Jane Grey passed through Traitor's Gate before meeting their tragic fates. The association of the White Tower with these executions and the infamous gateway solidified its reputation as a site of bloodshed.

The White Tower's chambers, including the dreaded Wakefield Tower, were used for torture and punishment. Prisoners were subjected to harsh interrogations and brutal treatment within its walls. Devices such as the rack, the scavenger's daughter, and the manacles were employed to extract confessions or to punish those deemed enemies of the state. The dark chambers and the instruments of torture further cemented the White Tower's association with violence and suffering.

The White Tower also became a backdrop for political intrigue and power struggles throughout history. From the Wars of the Roses to the Tudor era, the Tower witnessed intense power struggles and the rise and fall of influential figures. Imprisonment and execution within the Tower's walls were often politically motivated, serving as a means for those in power to eliminate their rivals or consolidate their authority. The White Tower became a tangible symbol of the monarchy's ability to assert control through force and intimidation.

The name "White Tower" belies the dark and violent history associated with this iconic structure. Its association with bloodshed, executions, torture, and political power struggles has solidified its reputation as a symbol of authority, brutality, and the monarchy's ability to wield absolute power. While the name may initially evoke images of grandeur and strength, it serves as a reminder of the harsh realities and human suffering that unfolded within its walls. The White Tower stands as a testament to the complexities of history, where beauty and bloodshed coexist, leaving an indelible mark on the Tower of London's legacy.

The Bloody Tower, a significant part of the Tower of London, carries a name that hints at the dark and gruesome events that have taken place within its walls. Over the years, reports of hauntings and paranormal occurrences have added to the chilling aura surrounding this historic tower. In this chapter, we explore the reported hauntings and supernatural phenomena associated with the Bloody Tower, delving into the eerie encounters and the enduring mysteries that shroud its dark past.

The Bloody Tower, originally known as the Garden Tower, was constructed in the late 13th century. Its association with bloodshed and tragedy stems from the events that unfolded within its confines. Notable historical figures, such as the Princes in the Tower and Sir Walter Raleigh, were imprisoned within the tower, leaving a lasting imprint on its haunted reputation.

One of the most enduring ghostly legends associated with the Bloody Tower involves the apparitions of the Princes in the Tower, Edward V and Richard, Duke of York. According to legend, their spirits roam the tower, forever seeking justice and peace. Witnesses have reported sightings of two young boys dressed in medieval clothing, evoking a sense of sorrow and tragedy. The ghostly presence of the Princes in the Tower adds to the eerie ambiance and haunting legacy of the Bloody Tower.

Another reported haunting within the Bloody Tower involves the presence of a ghostly lady. Witnesses have described encountering a spectral figure dressed in Tudor-era clothing, often believed to be the ghost of Lady Jane Grey. Lady Jane Grey, the Nine Days' Queen, was imprisoned within the Bloody Tower before her execution. Her ghostly manifestation adds to the atmosphere of sorrow and melancholy associated with the tower.

Poltergeist activity has been reported within the Bloody Tower, adding an element of unpredictability and unease. Witnesses have described objects moving inexplicably, doors slamming shut without cause, or unexplained knocking sounds. The source of this poltergeist activity remains a mystery, but it contributes to the paranormal reputation of the tower.

Visitors to the Bloody Tower have reported feelings of unease, discomfort, and unexplained cold spots. Some claim to have experienced a heavy and oppressive atmosphere, as if being watched by unseen entities. These sensations add to the unsettling ambiance within the tower, heightening the perception of its haunted nature.

Psychic investigators and sensitive individuals have described picking up psychic impressions or sensing residual energy within the Bloody Tower. They claim to feel the echoes of past traumas and emotional imprints left by the tower's dark history. Such experiences contribute to the notion that the Bloody Tower holds residual energy from its tragic past.

The Bloody Tower, with its haunting name and storied history, has become synonymous with tales of supernatural encounters and ghostly phenomena. The apparitions of the Princes in the Tower, the presence of a ghostly lady, poltergeist activity, feelings of unease, and psychic impressions all contribute to the tower's paranormal reputation. Whether these encounters are the result of overactive imaginations, psychological impressions, or genuine supernatural occurrences, they add to the chilling allure and enduring fascination surrounding the Bloody Tower. As visitors explore its dark corridors, they are reminded of the tragedies and sorrows that unfolded within its walls, leaving an indelible mark on its haunted legacy.

OLIVER LANCASTER

Chapter 6: The Traitor's Gate

T he Tower of London, with its foreboding walls and dark history, has a long-standing reputation as a place of imprisonment and torture. The imprisonment and entry of prisoners into the Tower, particularly through its infamous Traitor's Gate, played a significant role in the fortress's operations. In this chapter, we delve into the process of imprisoning and receiving prisoners within the Tower, exploring the procedures, symbolism, and conditions surrounding their captivity.

The Tower of London served as a prison for various categories of prisoners throughout its history. High-ranking nobles, political adversaries, and those accused of treason or other serious crimes were among the individuals incarcerated within its walls. Imprisonment in the Tower was seen as a mark of royal authority, emphasizing the power and control of the monarchy over their subjects.

When a prisoner arrived at the Tower, they were typically escorted through the city streets under heavy guard, their entry often marked by a procession that served to publicly display their fall from grace. Upon reaching the Tower, prisoners were met by the constable or the governor of the Tower and their staff, who took charge of the prisoners and oversaw their incarceration.

Traitor's Gate, located on the riverside of the Tower, played a central role in the entry of prisoners. The gate served as the entrance for prisoners arriving by boat, which was a common mode of transportation at the time. The prisoners were brought to the gate, often shackled and under close watch, before being escorted into the Tower's confines. Traitor's Gate symbolized the prisoners' descent into captivity, marking the end of their former lives and their entry into a realm of uncertainty and confinement.

The conditions of imprisonment within the Tower varied depending on the status and circumstances of the prisoners. Some were held in relative comfort, with access to private chambers, servants, and amenities. Others, particularly those accused of treason or political offenses, were confined to less luxurious quarters, such as the Beauchamp Tower or the Salt Tower. The conditions could be harsh, with limited space, lack of privacy, and restricted freedom.

Prisoners within the Tower were subject to interrogation and often faced intense questioning aimed at extracting information or eliciting confessions. The methods used during interrogations could range from persuasive tactics to harsher measures, including torture. The treatment of prisoners within the Tower varied, influenced by factors such as their social status, the nature of their alleged crimes, and the political climate of the time.

The imprisonment and entry of prisoners into the Tower were not merely administrative procedures but also symbolic acts. They served to demonstrate the power and authority of the monarchy, reinforcing the consequences of challenging royal rule. The public spectacle associated with the prisoners' arrival, the presence of guards, and the ceremonial procession aimed to publicly shame and humiliate the prisoners, further solidifying their position as enemies of the crown.

The Tower of London's role in the imprisonment and entry of prisoners was a significant aspect of its function as a fortress and a symbol of royal authority. The process of imprisonment, the symbolism associated with Traitor's Gate, the conditions of captivity, and the treatment of prisoners all contributed to the Tower's reputation as a place of fear and punishment. The imprisonment and public display of prisoners within the Tower served to reinforce the monarch's control, leaving a lasting impact on the collective memory and the haunting legacy of the Tower of London.

Traitor's Gate, the infamous entrance to the Tower of London, is steeped in history and tales of dark deeds. As the gateway through which prisoners were brought into the Tower, Traitor's Gate holds a reputation for being haunted and associated with spectral sightings. In this chapter, we explore the ghostly tales and reported sightings related to Traitor's Gate, delving into the eerie encounters and the enduring fascination surrounding this chilling entrance.

One of the most prominent ghostly tales associated with Traitor's Gate revolves around the spirit of Anne Boleyn, the ill-fated queen of Henry VIII. According to legend, her ghostly apparition has been seen near Traitor's Gate, as if forever trapped in her final journey to the Tower. Witnesses claim to have observed a spectral figure resembling Anne Boleyn, dressed in Tudor-era clothing, accompanied by an air of melancholy and tragedy. The haunting presence of Anne Boleyn adds to the ominous reputation of Traitor's Gate and the Tower of London.

Another eerie sighting related to Traitor's Gate involves the apparition of a ghostly figure in chains. Witnesses have reported encountering a spectral presence near the gate, wearing tattered and rusted chains that clank ominously as it moves. This haunting manifestation is believed to represent the tortured souls of those who suffered within the Tower, their captivity and suffering forever etched in the spiritual realm.

The Princes in the Tower, Edward V and Richard, Duke of York, who are associated with the Bloody Tower, also feature in ghostly tales related to Traitor's Gate. Legend has it that their ghostly apparitions have been seen near the gate, as if reliving their final moments before their mysterious disappearance. Witnesses claim to have glimpsed two young boys dressed in medieval clothing, evoking a sense of tragedy and sorrow. The presence of the Princes in the Tower adds to the haunting atmosphere and the enigma surrounding Traitor's Gate.

In addition to specific ghostly sightings, visitors to Traitor's Gate have reported feelings of unease, discomfort, and unexplained cold spots. Some claim to have experienced a sudden drop in temperature or a distinct chill in the air as they approach the gate. These sensations, combined with the knowledge of the gate's dark history, contribute to the unsettling ambiance and the perception of spiritual activity within its vicinity.

Psychics and sensitives who have visited Traitor's Gate have described picking up psychic impressions or sensing residual energy associated with the gate. They claim to feel the echoes of the emotional turmoil and trauma that accompanied the prisoners' arrival at the Tower. These psychic impressions contribute to the belief that the gate retains the residual energy of the fear, despair, and suffering that unfolded within its shadowy depths.

Traitor's Gate, as the foreboding entrance to the Tower of London, has become the subject of ghostly tales and reported sightings over the centuries. The apparitions of Anne Boleyn, the ghostly figure in chains, and the presence of the Princes in the Tower add to the haunting mystique surrounding the gate. Feelings of unease, cold spots, and psychic impressions further contribute to the eerie atmosphere associated with Traitor's Gate. Whether these encounters are attributed to overactive imaginations, psychological impressions, or genuine spiritual phenomena, they enhance the chilling reputation and enduring fascination surrounding this infamous entrance to the Tower of London.

OLIVER LANCASTER

Chapter 7: The Ravens of the Tower

———

One of the enduring beliefs associated with the Tower of London is the notion that its fate is tied to the presence of ravens within its walls. According to tradition, if the ravens were to leave the Tower, it would bring about its downfall. In this chapter, we explore the origins of this belief, the significance of the ravens, and the measures taken to safeguard their presence, highlighting the intriguing superstition surrounding the Tower's fate.

The legend of the Raven's Curse is deeply rooted in the folklore surrounding the Tower of London. The exact origins of this belief are uncertain, but it is said to date back centuries. According to the legend, Charles II, upon hearing a prophecy that the Tower would fall if the ravens were to depart, took steps to ensure their presence as protectors of the fortress.

The ravens have come to symbolize the Tower of London and are seen as the guardians of its security. Their presence is believed to protect the tower from destruction and safeguard the monarchy. The ravens' wings are clipped to prevent them from flying away, thus ensuring their continued presence within the Tower's grounds.

The tradition of caring for the ravens and upholding the Raven's Curse continues to this day. The Tower of London employs a team of Yeoman Warders, also known as the Beefeaters, who are responsible for the care and well-being of the ravens. The ravens are provided with food, shelter, and veterinary care, ensuring their health and contentment. Their wings are clipped as a precautionary measure, allowing them to roam freely within the Tower's confines.

The measures taken to protect the ravens are seen as essential to preserving the Tower's security. The belief in the Raven's Curse is deeply ingrained in the collective consciousness, and the superstition surrounding it is taken seriously. It is believed that if the ravens were to abandon the Tower, disaster would befall the fortress, and the monarchy would be at risk.

The legend of the Raven's Curse has captured the imagination of visitors to the Tower of London. The ravens have become iconic symbols of the fortress, drawing crowds who come to witness their presence and learn about the legend. The Tower's association with the ravens and the superstition surrounding them adds to the allure and mystique of this historic landmark.

The belief that the Tower of London would fall if the ravens were to leave is a captivating superstition that has captured the imagination of generations. The ravens have become more than mere birds; they are seen as guardians and protectors of the Tower's security. The legend and the measures taken to safeguard the ravens' presence add an element of mystery and fascination to the Tower's history. Whether seen as a charming superstition or an integral part of the Tower's cultural heritage, the Raven's Curse remains a cherished belief and a symbol of the enduring traditions associated with the Tower of London.

THE TOWER OF LONDON: THE HAUNTED PAST AND SECRETS OF ROYAL GHOSTS

The ravens of the Tower of London have long been associated with superstition and intrigue. Beyond their role in the Raven's Curse and their status as protectors of the Tower, the ravens have been the subject of supernatural and mysterious stories throughout history. In this chapter, we delve into some of these tales, exploring the enigmatic and otherworldly aspects of the ravens that have captured the imagination of visitors and locals alike.

According to folklore, the ravens of the Tower possess the ability to shape-shift into other forms. Some tales speak of the ravens transforming into other creatures or even taking on human-like appearances. These accounts add an element of mystery and enchantment to the ravens' presence, suggesting a connection to ancient myths and legends where shape-shifting beings played prominent roles.

There have been claims of individuals communicating with the ravens of the Tower. Some assert that they have been able to understand the ravens' calls or even engage in telepathic communication with them. While these accounts may be seen as products of vivid imagination or spiritual connection, they contribute to the mystical reputation of the ravens and their perceived intelligence.

In certain instances, the ravens of the Tower have been said to exhibit behavior that foretells significant events or changes. Some believe that the ravens become restless or exhibit unusual behavior before significant events, such as the passing of a monarch or a major historical event. These accounts, although subjective and open to interpretation, add an element of mystery and divination to the ravens' presence within the Tower.

There have been occasional reports of mysterious disappearances of ravens from the Tower. Some claim that the ravens have inexplicably vanished without any apparent explanation. These incidents have given rise to speculation and intrigue, leading to theories about supernatural forces, curses, or hidden realms beyond our understanding. While these disappearances may have mundane explanations, they contribute to the sense of mystery surrounding the ravens.

In folklore, the ravens of the Tower have been depicted as guardians of the fortress's secrets and hidden knowledge. It is believed that they possess a deep understanding of the Tower's history and are privy to hidden realms or mystical realms within its walls. This portrayal adds an air of mysticism to the ravens, positioning them as keepers of ancient wisdom and guardians of the Tower's enigmatic past.

The ravens of the Tower of London have captivated the imagination of people for centuries. Beyond their role in the Raven's Curse and their guardianship of the Tower, the ravens have been the subjects of supernatural and mysterious stories. Tales of shapeshifting, communication, foretelling of events, mysterious disappearances, and guardianship of secrets have added to the allure and intrigue surrounding these majestic birds. Whether viewed as folklore, imaginative tales, or glimpses into the mystical nature of the ravens, these stories contribute to the sense of wonder and fascination associated with the Tower of London and its enigmatic residents.

THE TOWER OF LONDON: THE HAUNTED PAST AND SECRETS OF ROYAL GHOSTS

Chapter 8: The Crown Jewels and Their Guardians

The ravens of the Tower of London hold a special place in the fortress's history and folklore. As protectors of the Tower, their well-being and presence are of utmost importance. In this chapter, we explore the storage and protection of the Tower's ravens, shedding light on the measures taken to ensure their safety and the significance of their role within the fortress.

The Tower's ravens are provided with suitable housing within the confines of the fortress. They have their own dedicated enclosure, known as the Raven's Lodge, where they can seek shelter and rest. The Raven's Lodge offers a secure and comfortable space for the ravens, equipped with perches, nesting areas, and other amenities to accommodate their needs. While they have a designated enclosure, the ravens are also allowed to roam freely within the Tower's grounds during the day, allowing them to exercise and explore their surroundings.

The care of the ravens is entrusted to the Yeoman Warders, also known as the Beefeaters, who have been responsible for the welfare of the ravens for centuries. The ravens are fed a diet that meets their nutritional requirements, consisting of high-quality meat, fruits, and other suitable foods. The Yeoman Warders ensure that the ravens receive regular and appropriate meals, keeping them healthy and well-nourished.

Additionally, veterinary care is provided whenever necessary to maintain their well-being.

To prevent the ravens from flying away from the Tower, a precautionary measure is taken: their wings are clipped. Trained professionals carefully trim the flight feathers to limit their ability to take flight. This practice ensures that the ravens remain within the Tower's confines and do not venture too far from their designated area. Clipping the wings allows for the continued presence of the ravens within the Tower and upholds the tradition associated with the Raven's Curse.

The Tower's ravens are protected from harm and potential threats. Their enclosure is designed to be secure, preventing predators or unwanted intruders from gaining access. The Yeoman Warders closely monitor the ravens, ensuring their safety and promptly addressing any issues that may arise. The protection of the ravens is considered a priority, as they are seen as integral to the Tower's history, folklore, and the superstitious beliefs associated with their presence.

The storage and protection of the Tower's ravens go beyond their physical well-being. Their presence within the Tower carries cultural significance and symbolizes the enduring traditions and folklore associated with this historic landmark. By providing proper care and protection for the ravens, the Tower of London upholds these traditions and preserves the unique connection between the ravens, the fortress, and its history.

THE TOWER OF LONDON: THE HAUNTED PAST AND SECRETS OF ROYAL GHOSTS

The storage and protection of the Tower's ravens are essential aspects of maintaining their presence within the fortress. Through suitable housing, proper feeding and care, the clipping of wings, and protection from harm, the Tower ensures the well-being and continued presence of the ravens. Beyond their physical needs, the storage and protection of the ravens uphold the cultural significance and traditions associated with their role as protectors of the Tower. By safeguarding the ravens, the Tower of London maintains a connection to its past and perpetuates the enchanting folklore that surrounds these remarkable birds.

The Crown Jewels of the United Kingdom, housed within the Tower of London, are among the most revered and precious treasures in the world. Alongside the splendor and historical significance of the Crown Jewels, paranormal experiences and mysterious occurrences have been reported by both visitors and guardians. In this chapter, we delve into the intriguing tales and paranormal encounters related to the Crown Jewels and those tasked with their protection.

One of the most enduring paranormal tales associated with the Crown Jewels involves the ghostly apparitions of their guardians. The Yeoman Warders, responsible for protecting the Crown Jewels, have reported sightings and encounters with spectral figures within the Jewel House. Witnesses describe encountering ghostly sentinels in historic uniforms, standing vigilantly near the jewels, their presence evoking a sense of duty and dedication even in the afterlife. These ghostly encounters add to the mystique and reverence surrounding the Crown Jewels.

Visitors to the Jewel House have reported experiencing eerie sensations and unexplained phenomena when in the presence of the Crown Jewels. Some claim to have felt a profound sense of awe, as if being watched by unseen eyes or engulfed in an ethereal presence. Others have reported hearing whispers or feeling a chilling breeze despite being indoors. These encounters with the Crown Jewels and their related artifacts suggest a connection to the spiritual realm and the potential lingering energy surrounding these treasures.

The Koh-i-Noor diamond, one of the most famous gems in the Crown Jewels, is steeped in legend and superstition. It is believed to carry a curse, bringing misfortune to its male possessors. Some claim that paranormal events and tragedies have befallen those who have owned or worn the diamond, adding to its enigmatic reputation. While these occurrences cannot be definitively linked to the paranormal, they contribute to the notion that certain objects within the Crown Jewels possess an otherworldly aura.

There have been reports of ghostly celebrations and merriment within the Jewel House during the night. Witnesses claim to have heard faint music, laughter, and the clinking of glasses emanating from the area where the Crown Jewels are displayed. These ethereal sounds suggest the presence of joyous spirits, perhaps celebrating the magnificence and historical significance of the Crown Jewels. While the origins of these spectral celebrations remain unknown, they add an intriguing layer of mystery to the paranormal experiences surrounding the jewels.

Psychics and sensitives who have visited the Jewel House have described picking up psychic impressions and sensing residual energies associated with the Crown Jewels. They claim to feel echoes of the past, picking up on the emotions and energies imprinted on these precious artifacts throughout their long history. These psychic impressions offer a glimpse into the rich tapestry of human experiences and emotions that are intertwined with the Crown Jewels.

The Crown Jewels of the Tower of London, as symbols of regal splendor and historical significance, are not exempt from tales of the paranormal. Ghostly encounters with the guardians, eerie sensations, haunted artifacts, and reports of spectral celebrations contribute to the fascination and mystique surrounding the Crown Jewels. While some experiences may be attributed to overactive imaginations or psychological impressions, others hint at a connection to the spiritual realm and the profound emotions associated with these treasures. The paranormal encounters related to the Crown Jewels add to their allure, inviting us to contemplate the mysteries that lie beyond the tangible beauty and historical importance of these remarkable artifacts.

OLIVER LANCASTER

Chapter 9: The Chapel Royal of St. Peter ad Vincula

───

The Tower of London holds a unique and significant place in history, intertwined with the identity and legacy of the city of London and the monarchy. In this chapter, we explore the historical importance of the Tower and its deep connection to the fortress, delving into its role as a symbol of power, a center of governance, and a witness to pivotal events that shaped the course of English and British history.

Throughout its history, the Tower of London has stood as a symbol of power and authority. Its imposing structure and strategic location on the banks of the River Thames made it a formidable stronghold, conveying the might and control of the monarchy. As a symbol of royal power, the Tower served as a reminder to the populace of the monarch's ability to protect and govern, while also serving as a deterrent to potential adversaries.

The Tower of London has played a central role in governance throughout the centuries. It served as a royal palace, a treasury, and an armory, functioning as a hub for administrative and ceremonial activities. The monarch and their court resided within its walls, and important state functions and events were held within its grand halls. The Tower's significance as a center of governance highlights its role as the heart of royal authority and decision-making.

The Tower of London has witnessed and played a part in pivotal events that shaped English and British history. From the Wars of the Roses to the execution of monarchs, the Tower has been the stage for moments of triumph and tragedy. It has seen the rise and fall of powerful figures, political intrigue, and acts of rebellion. The Tower's historical importance lies not only in its physical structure but also in its connection to these transformative events that shaped the nation's destiny.

The Tower of London's significance extends beyond its historical and political importance. It also serves as a custodian of cultural heritage. The Crown Jewels, housed within its walls, represent centuries of craftsmanship and regal splendor. The architecture, artwork, and artifacts within the Tower provide valuable insights into the past, offering a tangible link to the rich tapestry of British history and identity.

Today, the Tower of London stands as one of the most visited landmarks in the United Kingdom, attracting millions of tourists each year. Its historical importance, combined with its mysterious legends and iconic features, has made it an enduring symbol of the nation. The Tower's draw as a tourist attraction allows visitors to immerse themselves in the stories and experiences that have unfolded within its walls, further enhancing its cultural and historical significance.

The Tower of London's historical importance and its deep connection to the fortress are undeniable. It has served as a symbol of power and authority, a center of governance, and a witness to pivotal events that shaped English and British history. Through its preservation of cultural heritage and its role as a tourist attraction, the Tower continues to captivate and educate visitors, fostering an appreciation for the nation's past. The Tower of London stands not only as an architectural marvel but also as a living testament to the rich tapestry of human experiences and the enduring legacy of the monarchy and the nation it represents.

The chapel within the Tower of London, known as the Tower Chapel or the Chapel Royal of St. Peter ad Vincula, holds a rich history and is steeped in spirituality. Throughout the years, numerous ghostly encounters and legends have emerged, adding to its mystique and eerie reputation. In this chapter, we delve into the ghostly tales and legends associated with the Tower Chapel, uncovering the spectral sightings and unexplained phenomena that have fascinated visitors and caretakers alike.

One of the most prominent ghostly encounters associated with the Tower Chapel involves the apparition of Anne Boleyn, the ill-fated queen of Henry VIII. According to legend, her spirit has been seen near the chapel, sometimes kneeling in prayer or pacing restlessly. Witnesses have described a figure dressed in a white gown, evoking a sense of sorrow and tragedy. The presence of Anne Boleyn's ghost adds to the somber atmosphere and haunting allure of the Tower Chapel.

Another haunting legend linked to the Tower Chapel revolves around Lady Jane Grey, the "Nine Days' Queen." Legend has it that her ghostly procession is seen in the vicinity of the chapel, as if reenacting her final journey to the executioner's block. Witnesses claim to have observed a spectral procession of figures dressed in Tudor-era clothing, accompanied by a solemn atmosphere and a sense of foreboding. The ghostly procession of Lady Jane Grey adds to the eerie ambiance and tragic history associated with the Tower Chapel.

Visitors to the Tower Chapel have reported hearing strange voices and whispers, even when the chapel is empty. Some claim to have heard faint prayers, chanting, or murmurs echoing through the sacred space. These mysterious auditory phenomena contribute to the belief that the chapel retains the residual energy and spiritual presence of its past inhabitants. The whispers in the chapel add to its mysticism and evoke a sense of the ethereal realm.

There have been accounts of cold spots and eerie sensations experienced by individuals within the Tower Chapel. Some visitors claim to have encountered sudden drops in temperature, even on warm days, as if entering a spectral realm. Others describe feelings of unease, heaviness, or being watched by unseen eyes. These paranormal sensations heighten the sense of the chapel's haunted nature and the presence of lingering spirits.

Psychics and sensitives who have visited the Tower Chapel have described picking up psychic impressions and sensing spiritual energies within its walls. They claim to feel the emotional imprints and echoes of the past, perceiving the prayers, grief, and spiritual devotion of those who worshipped within the chapel. These impressions contribute to the belief that the chapel acts as a conduit for spiritual energy and serves as a bridge between the earthly and the ethereal.

THE TOWER OF LONDON: THE HAUNTED PAST AND SECRETS OF ROYAL GHOSTS

The Tower Chapel, with its rich history and spiritual significance, has become a focal point for ghostly encounters and legends within the Tower of London. The spectral figures of Anne Boleyn and Lady Jane Grey, the mysterious voices and whispers, the cold spots, and the psychic impressions all contribute to the haunting reputation of the chapel. Whether these encounters are attributed to overactive imaginations, psychological impressions, or genuine spiritual phenomena, they enhance the chilling allure and enduring fascination surrounding the Tower Chapel. As visitors step into its sacred space, they are reminded of the spiritual legacy and the enigmatic connection between the mortal realm and the realm of the supernatural.

OLIVER LANCASTER

Chapter 10: Notable Prisoners of the Tower

———

T he Tower of London has served as a place of confinement for a diverse array of prisoners throughout history. From high-ranking nobles to political adversaries, individuals accused of treason, and those who fell out of favor with the monarchy, the Tower's cells have witnessed a multitude of stories, crimes, and fates. In this chapter, we explore the lives, alleged crimes, and ultimate fates of some notable prisoners who endured captivity within the Tower's formidable walls.

Sir Walter Raleigh, a prominent figure during the reign of Queen Elizabeth I, found himself imprisoned within the Tower on multiple occasions. Raleigh was accused of treason for his alleged involvement in a plot against King James I. Despite his literary accomplishments and exploration endeavors, Raleigh's reputation as a schemer and conspirator led to his imprisonment. After years of confinement, he was eventually released but was later executed under different charges.

Guy Fawkes, along with his co-conspirators, plotted to blow up the Houses of Parliament in what became known as the Gunpowder Plot of 1605. Fawkes was captured while guarding the barrels of gunpowder hidden beneath the House of Lords. He was subsequently brought to the Tower, where he endured interrogation and torture. Fawkes and his fellow conspirators were ultimately executed for their crimes, with Fawkes meeting his fate through the gruesome method of being hanged, drawn, and quartered.

Anne Boleyn, the second wife of King Henry VIII, is one of the most famous prisoners associated with the Tower of London. Accused of adultery and treason, Anne Boleyn was imprisoned in the Tower before her trial and execution. Her alleged crimes included plotting against the king and engaging in extramarital affairs. Despite her protests of innocence, Anne Boleyn was found guilty and beheaded within the confines of the Tower, leaving a haunting legacy and a tale of tragic fate.

Lady Jane Grey, also known as the "Nine Days' Queen," faced a brief but tragic reign as the queen of England. Following the death of Edward VI, Lady Jane Grey was proclaimed queen but faced resistance from supporters of Mary Tudor. She was imprisoned within the Tower and later charged with treason. Despite her youth and lack of agency in her ascension to the throne, Lady Jane Grey was executed at a young age, marking a poignant and unjust fate.

During World War II, the Tower of London held a prisoner of a different era. Rudolf Hess, Adolf Hitler's deputy, crash-landed in Scotland in an attempt to negotiate peace with the British government. Instead, he was arrested and subsequently brought to the Tower. Hess spent several weeks as a prisoner before being transferred to other locations. His imprisonment within the Tower stands as a testament to the significance of the fortress even in more recent historical contexts.

THE TOWER OF LONDON: THE HAUNTED PAST AND SECRETS OF ROYAL GHOSTS

The Tower of London's history is intertwined with the stories, crimes, and ultimate fates of numerous prisoners who found themselves confined within its walls. From political conspirators like Guy Fawkes and treasonous queens like Anne Boleyn to explorers like Sir Walter Raleigh and war-era prisoners like Rudolf Hess, the Tower's cells have housed individuals from various walks of life and historical contexts. Their stories and fates, marked by intrigue, tragedy, and the weight of political power, serve as reminders of the Tower's role as a place of confinement and punishment throughout the ages.

The Tower of London's long history as a place of imprisonment and execution has given rise to numerous tales of ghostly manifestations and haunting accounts. Many of these stories revolve around the prisoners who endured captivity within the Tower's walls. In this chapter, we delve into reported ghostly encounters and haunting accounts associated with notable prisoners, exploring the spectral presence that lingers within the fortress's confines.

Anne Boleyn, the ill-fated queen of Henry VIII, is one of the most famous prisoners associated with the Tower of London. It is said that her ghostly presence haunts the Tower, specifically the areas where she was held in captivity. Witnesses have reported sightings of a spectral figure resembling Anne Boleyn, dressed in Tudor-era clothing, often seen near the chapel or in the White Tower. Her ghostly apparition is accompanied by an air of sadness and tragedy, forever trapped in the place where her life came to a violent end.

The ghosts of the Gunpowder Plot conspirators, including Guy Fawkes and his co-conspirators, are said to haunt the Tower. There have been accounts of ghostly figures seen in the Beauchamp Tower, where the plotters were held during their interrogations. Witnesses have described apparitions dressed in period clothing, sometimes displaying signs of torture. The haunting presence of these spectral figures serves as a reminder of the consequences of their failed plot and the grisly fate that awaited them.

Lady Jane Grey, the "Nine Days' Queen," is believed to be among the restless spirits that roam the Tower. It is said that her ghostly figure can be seen in the area near the Chapel Royal of St. Peter ad Vincula, where she was executed. Witnesses have reported sightings of a young woman dressed in Tudor attire, evoking a sense of melancholy and tragic destiny. Lady Jane Grey's spirit serves as a haunting reminder of her brief and ill-fated reign.

While many notable prisoners have left their spectral imprint on the Tower, there are countless unnamed individuals who suffered and perished within its walls. The Tower's dark past and extensive history as a place of confinement have led to reports of tormented souls and restless spirits haunting various areas. Visitors and caretakers have described sensations of being watched, unexplained noises, and cold spots that hint at the presence of these unidentified prisoners.

Sir Walter Raleigh, known for his expeditions and political intrigue, is believed to have left an otherworldly mark on the Tower. Witnesses have reported encountering a ghostly figure resembling Raleigh, often seen near the Bloody Tower or in the Byward Tower. His apparition is described as wearing period clothing and exuding an air of intelligence and charisma. The spirit of Sir Walter Raleigh is seen as a reminder of the Tower's complex history and the remarkable individuals who endured captivity within its walls.

The Tower of London, with its dark and storied past, has become synonymous with tales of ghostly manifestations and haunting accounts. The spirits of Anne Boleyn, the Gunpowder Plot conspirators, Lady Jane Grey, and Sir Walter Raleigh are among the notable prisoners believed to haunt the Tower. These spectral figures serve as a reminder of the Tower's haunting legacy and the echoes of the past that continue to reverberate within its formidable walls. The reported ghostly encounters and haunting accounts add to the enigma and allure of the Tower, inviting visitors to contemplate the profound human experiences and tragedies that unfolded within its confines.

OLIVER LANCASTER

Chapter 11: The Torture Tower

───────

The Tower of London, known for its role as a place of imprisonment and punishment, has witnessed a range of brutal methods of torture throughout its history. From extracting confessions to inflicting excruciating pain, these methods were designed to extract information or punish those accused of crimes. In this chapter, we explore some of the specific methods of torture employed within the Tower's walls, shedding light on the dark practices that unfolded within its confines.

One of the most infamous torture devices used in the Tower was the rack. The victim would be stretched out on a wooden frame while ropes or chains were attached to their limbs. The device was then tightened, exerting excruciating pressure on the victim's joints and muscles. The rack was used to elicit confessions or to punish individuals deemed as threats to the monarchy. The agonizing pain inflicted by the rack made it a terrifying and effective tool of torture.

The Scavenger's Daughter, also known as the Skeffington's Gyve, was a device invented during the Tudor era. It consisted of a metal hoop and iron shackles that encased the victim, forcing them into a crouched position. The device would then be tightened, compressing the victim's body and inflicting unbearable pain. The Scavenger's Daughter was specifically designed to crush the body inward, making it one of the most agonizing forms of torture used within the Tower.

The Tower's dungeons were equipped with manacles and chains, which were used to restrain prisoners. The captives would have their hands or feet shackled, often in uncomfortable positions, and then chained to the walls or floors. This method of torture not only caused physical discomfort but also restricted movement, making it difficult for prisoners to find any semblance of comfort or rest. The psychological torment of being confined in this manner added to the overall suffering endured by those held captive.

Water torture was a method commonly employed in the Tower and elsewhere during interrogations. It involved strapping the victim to a chair or table and repeatedly pouring water over their face, causing a sensation of suffocation and drowning. This form of torture was designed to elicit confessions or extract information from prisoners. The fear and terror induced by the sensation of drowning made water torture a highly effective and psychologically damaging method.

The boot was a brutal instrument of torture used within the Tower. The victim's leg would be secured within a wooden or metal contraption, and wedges or bars would be driven into it using a mallet. The pressure exerted on the leg would crush bones, shatter limbs, and cause excruciating pain. The boot was employed to punish individuals or to extract information, leaving the victim permanently maimed and scarred.

THE TOWER OF LONDON: THE HAUNTED PAST AND SECRETS OF ROYAL GHOSTS

The Tower of London's history is marred by the use of various methods of torture, aimed at inflicting pain, eliciting confessions, and punishing prisoners. The rack, the Scavenger's Daughter, manacles and chains, water torture, and the boot represent just a few examples of the brutal practices that were employed within the Tower's walls. These methods of torture reveal the grim and inhumane nature of the Tower's role as a place of punishment and the suffering endured by those who fell into its clutches. Today, these dark practices serve as a haunting reminder of the Tower's dark past and the immense human cost of seeking power or challenging the authority of the monarchy.

The Torture Tower, also known as the Wakefield Tower, within the Tower of London holds a notorious reputation for its dark history and the brutal practices that took place within its walls. Over the years, reports of paranormal activities and hauntings have emerged, suggesting that the echoes of suffering and torment continue to resonate within this eerie space. In this chapter, we delve into the reported paranormal activities and hauntings associated with the Torture Tower, uncovering the chilling encounters and unexplained phenomena that have captured the imagination of visitors and caretakers.

Witnesses have reported encountering spectral apparitions within the Torture Tower. These ghostly figures are often described as tormented souls, clad in tattered and bloodstained clothing, evoking the pain and anguish suffered within its confines. Some accounts mention the apparitions of prisoners, their faces etched with fear and agony, serving as haunting reminders of the horrors that transpired within the Torture Tower.

Unexplained sounds and voices have been reported emanating from the Torture Tower. Visitors and caretakers have described hearing chilling screams, moans, and whispers, as if the tortured spirits of the past still linger within its walls. These auditory phenomena contribute to the unsettling atmosphere of the Torture Tower, heightening the sense of the supernatural and invoking a feeling of unease.

Visitors to the Torture Tower have experienced sudden drops in temperature and unexplained sensations of being watched or touched by unseen hands. These cold spots and eerie sensations are often associated with paranormal activity and are believed to be a result of the residual energy and spiritual presence that remain within the Torture Tower. The chilling cold and inexplicable touch serve as a chilling reminder of the torment endured by prisoners in this grim space.

Reports have surfaced of objects being disturbed or moved within the Torture Tower without any logical explanation. Visitors have witnessed doors opening and closing on their own, chains rattling without apparent cause, and shadows moving along the walls. These occurrences contribute to the sense of a restless energy that permeates the Torture Tower, leaving visitors with a sense of awe and apprehension.

Psychics and sensitives who have visited the Torture Tower claim to pick up on psychic impressions and emotional residue from the past. They describe feeling overwhelming emotions of fear, anguish, and despair, as if they are tapping into the residual energy left behind by the victims of torture. These impressions serve as a chilling reminder of the immense suffering that occurred within the Torture Tower and the lasting impact it has had on the spiritual realm.

The Torture Tower within the Tower of London stands as a stark reminder of the brutal practices and human suffering that took place within its walls. Reports of paranormal activities and hauntings within the Torture Tower add to its chilling allure and the sense of a lingering presence from the past. Spectral apparitions, eerie sounds and voices, cold spots, disturbed objects, and psychic impressions all contribute to the haunted reputation of this grim space. As visitors venture into the Torture Tower, they are confronted with the chilling echoes of a dark history, heightening their awareness of the enduring legacy of torment and despair within the Tower of London.

OLIVER LANCASTER

Chapter 12: The Execution Site

The Tower of London has witnessed numerous executions throughout its history, as it served as a site of punishment and the final destination for many condemned individuals. From high-ranking nobles to political adversaries and individuals accused of treason, the Tower's execution sites have witnessed the passing of significant figures. In this chapter, we explore some of the notable executions that took place within the Tower's walls, delving into the stories, circumstances, and legacies of those who met their fate at the hands of the executioner.

Perhaps one of the most famous and controversial executions associated with the Tower of London is that of Anne Boleyn, the second wife of King Henry VIII. Accused of adultery, treason, and conspiring against the king, Anne Boleyn was beheaded within the Tower's confines on May 19, 1536. Her execution marked a pivotal moment in English history and has left a lasting legacy, making her one of the Tower's most enduring figures.

Lady Jane Grey, also known as the "Nine Days' Queen," faced a tragic fate within the Tower. Following a brief reign as the queen of England, she was accused of treason and imprisoned in the Tower. Despite her youth and lack of agency in her ascension to the throne, Lady Jane Grey was executed on February 12, 1554. Her execution symbolized the volatile nature of Tudor politics and the harsh consequences faced by those caught in the power struggles of the time.

In the aftermath of the failed Gunpowder Plot of 1605, Guy Fawkes and his co-conspirators met their end within the Tower's walls. Fawkes, along with several others, was found guilty of treason for his involvement in the plot to blow up the Houses of Parliament. They were executed by hanging, drawing, and quartering, a brutal and gruesome method of execution. The Gunpowder Plot conspirators' fate serves as a reminder of the consequences faced by those who sought to challenge the existing political order.

William Wallace, the Scottish knight and military leader, was captured and brought to the Tower of London in 1305. Accused of high treason against the English crown, Wallace endured a trial and was subsequently executed. His execution, which involved hanging, drawing, and quartering, aimed to serve as a warning to those who would challenge English rule. Although Wallace's execution took place centuries ago, his defiance and legacy continue to resonate in Scottish history.

Sir Thomas More, the renowned scholar and statesman, was executed within the Tower's walls in 1535. More's refusal to recognize King Henry VIII as the head of the Church of England led to charges of treason. Despite his unwavering principles and esteemed reputation, More was convicted and executed by beheading. His execution stands as a poignant reminder of the religious and political upheavals of the Tudor era.

THE TOWER OF LONDON: THE HAUNTED PAST AND SECRETS OF ROYAL GHOSTS

The Tower of London's execution sites have witnessed the passing of numerous notable individuals throughout history. From Anne Boleyn's dramatic downfall to the tragic fate of Lady Jane Grey and the consequences faced by the Gunpowder Plot conspirators, these executions highlight the tumultuous nature of politics, power, and religious conflicts in different eras. The stories and legacies of those who met their end within the Tower's walls continue to captivate and resonate, leaving an indelible mark on the Tower's historical narrative and the collective memory of the nation.

The execution site within the Tower of London holds a somber and chilling atmosphere, bearing witness to the final moments of condemned individuals throughout history. It is within this haunting space that reports of ghostly apparitions and eerie experiences have emerged. In this chapter, we delve into the accounts of paranormal encounters and unsettling phenomena at the execution site, exploring the lingering presence and spectral echoes of those who met their demise in this solemn place.

Witnesses have reported encountering spectral figures and apparitions at the execution site within the Tower of London. These ghostly manifestations are often described as shadowy forms or translucent figures dressed in period clothing, evoking the haunting presence of those who met their fate at this site. Visitors have claimed to see ethereal figures standing upon the scaffold, as if reliving the moment of their execution, their energy forever imprinted within the fabric of the Tower.

Many individuals who have visited the execution site have reported experiencing intense feelings of unease, sadness, or a heavy sense of oppression. The air itself seems charged with a palpable energy that weighs upon visitors, evoking a sense of foreboding and sorrow. These unsettling emotions contribute to the chilling atmosphere of the execution site, leaving an indelible impression on those who dare to tread upon this hallowed ground.

Visitors to the execution site have described hearing muffled cries, phantom sounds, or inexplicable noises. Some report hearing disembodied voices whispering, the clanking of chains, or the sound of footsteps upon the scaffold. These auditory phenomena add to the eerie ambiance of the execution site, suggesting that the echoes of the past continue to reverberate within the walls, forever etching their presence upon the senses of those who bear witness.

Cold spots, sudden drops in temperature, and unexplained sensations have been reported at the execution site. Visitors describe feelings of being watched, touched, or a sense of being enveloped by an unseen presence. These paranormal encounters contribute to the notion that the spirits of the condemned linger within this space, seeking solace or perhaps perpetually trapped in their final moments.

Psychics and sensitives who have visited the execution site claim to pick up on psychic impressions and emotional residue. They describe feeling overwhelmed by emotions such as fear, sadness, or anger, as if tapping into the residual energy left behind by the individuals who faced their ultimate fate at this site. These impressions serve as a chilling reminder of the emotional intensity and profound human experiences that unfolded upon the scaffold.

The execution site within the Tower of London stands as a place of profound historical significance and poignant remembrance. Reports of ghostly apparitions, eerie experiences, and unexplained phenomena add to the haunting allure of this solemn space. The spectral figures, oppressive atmosphere, phantom sounds, cold spots, and psychic impressions evoke a sense of the lingering presence and spiritual energy that resides within the execution site. As visitors stand in this chilling space, they are reminded of the enduring echoes of the past and the powerful legacy of those who met their fate upon the scaffold, forever imprinting their mark upon the Tower's history.

OLIVER LANCASTER

Chapter 13: The Royal Menagerie

B eyond its role as a fortress, prison, and royal residence, the Tower of London has also been home to a menagerie of exotic animals throughout history. These creatures, often bestowed as gifts or collected for their rarity and novelty, added an element of fascination and splendor to the Tower's diverse functions. In this chapter, we explore the presence of exotic animals within the Tower, delving into the stories of lions, elephants, polar bears, and other fascinating creatures that once roamed its grounds.

The Royal Menagerie, established in the early 13th century, housed a diverse collection of exotic animals within the Tower of London. Its purpose was to showcase the wealth, power, and global reach of the British monarchy. The menagerie became a source of fascination for both royalty and the general public, attracting visitors from far and wide who were eager to witness these rare and exotic creatures.

Lions were among the most iconic and captivating animals housed within the Tower. The kings and queens of England maintained a fascination with lions, and these majestic beasts symbolized their power and authority. The sight of lions roaming the grounds of the Tower captured the imagination of visitors and served as a visual representation of the monarchy's dominion over both land and wildlife.

Elephants were another notable presence in the Tower's menagerie. These magnificent creatures, with their imposing size and graceful demeanor, were highly prized for their rarity. Elephants were often gifted to the English monarchs by foreign dignitaries and rulers. They became objects of curiosity and wonder, captivating the attention of both royal spectators and commoners alike.

Polar bears, native to the Arctic, were also among the exotic animals kept within the Tower. Their appearance in London was met with great intrigue, as they were considered strange and fascinating creatures from distant lands. Polar bears were seen as symbols of exploration and adventure, reflecting the maritime ambitions and global reach of the British Empire.

In addition to lions, elephants, and polar bears, the Tower of London housed a wide array of exotic animals over the years. These included leopards, camels, kangaroos, ostriches, and various species of birds. Each addition to the menagerie brought an element of novelty and spectacle, providing entertainment and education for those who had the opportunity to witness these remarkable creatures up close.

The presence of exotic animals within the Tower gradually diminished over time. As the understanding of animal welfare evolved, the conditions in which these animals were kept came under scrutiny. Eventually, the Royal Menagerie was disbanded, and the remaining animals were relocated to other locations, including the London Zoo, where they could be cared for in more suitable environments.

THE TOWER OF LONDON: THE HAUNTED PAST AND SECRETS OF ROYAL GHOSTS

The Tower of London's history encompasses not only its role as a fortress and place of confinement but also as a home for exotic animals from around the world. Lions, elephants, polar bears, and a diverse assortment of creatures once graced the Tower's grounds, capturing the imagination and curiosity of all who had the privilege of seeing them. These exotic animals symbolized the majesty, power, and global reach of the British monarchy, leaving a legacy of wonder and fascination that continues to captivate our imaginations today.

The Tower Menagerie, once home to a collection of exotic animals within the Tower of London, holds a unique place in its storied history. The presence of these remarkable creatures has sparked tales of ghostly encounters and legends that continue to intrigue visitors and caretakers of the Tower. In this chapter, we delve into the reported ghostly encounters and legends associated with the Tower Menagerie, unraveling the spectral tales and mysterious phenomena that surround these extraordinary animals.

One of the most prevalent legends surrounding the Tower Menagerie involves the ghostly roar of lions. Visitors and caretakers have reported hearing phantom roars echoing through the corridors and grounds of the Tower. These otherworldly sounds, reminiscent of the majestic beasts that once inhabited the menagerie, contribute to the eerie ambiance and perpetuate the belief that the spirits of these lions still roam their former domain.

Legend has it that the spirits of the exotic animals once housed in the Tower Menagerie continue to wander the grounds.

Witnesses claim to have seen ghostly forms of lions, elephants, and other creatures gliding through the Tower's courtyards and enclosures. These spectral apparitions, often described as translucent or ethereal, add an air of enchantment and mystique to the Tower, leaving visitors in awe of the spectral presence of these magnificent creatures.

Some reports suggest encounters with phantom zookeepers and handlers associated with the Tower Menagerie. Visitors and staff have described seeing figures dressed in period attire, tending to the invisible animals or going about their duties as if they were still caring for the exotic creatures. These ghostly encounters lend credence to the belief that the spirits of the menagerie's keepers continue to watch over the animals, even in the afterlife.

It is said that the restless spirits of the menagerie's animals manifest in various ways within the Tower. Visitors have reported hearing the phantom sounds of elephants trumpeting, lions growling, and the screeches of other creatures, as if their spirits yearn to break free from their spectral confines. These eerie auditory experiences evoke a sense of wonder and curiosity, inviting visitors to contemplate the enduring presence of the animals' spirits.

Psychics and sensitives who have visited the Tower Menagerie claim to have picked up on psychic impressions and residual energy associated with the animals. They describe feeling a vibrant energy, a sense of vitality and longing that lingers in the spaces where the menagerie once thrived. These impressions serve as a testament to the deep connection between humans and animals, suggesting that the bond formed in life extends beyond the grave.

The Tower Menagerie, with its collection of exotic animals, has left an indelible mark on the history and legends of the Tower of London. The ghostly encounters and legends surrounding the menagerie infuse the Tower with an air of mystery and enchantment. From the ghostly roars of lions to the spectral apparitions of animals and phantom zookeepers, these accounts add depth to the legacy of the menagerie's inhabitants. As visitors explore the Tower's grounds, they may find themselves captivated by the ethereal presence of these extraordinary creatures, forever etched in the tapestry of the Tower's paranormal lore.

OLIVER LANCASTER

Chapter 14: The Tower as a Tourist Attraction

The Tower of London, once a place of confinement and regal authority, has undergone a transformation over the years, evolving into a popular tourist attraction. Opening its doors to the public has allowed visitors to delve into its rich history, marvel at its architectural splendor, and immerse themselves in the intriguing stories that have unfolded within its walls. In this chapter, we explore the Tower's opening to the public and its significant role in tourism, becoming a cherished destination for both locals and international visitors.

In the 19th century, the Tower of London began to welcome visitors, marking the transition from its primary role as a fortress and prison to a cultural and historical landmark. Its grandeur, rich heritage, and captivating legends attracted individuals seeking to immerse themselves in the tapestry of English history. The Tower's unique combination of architectural magnificence, royal connections, and macabre tales created an irresistible allure that resonated with both local residents and global tourists.

The Tower's opening to the public brought with it an opportunity for educational enrichment and historical exploration. Visitors could wander through the ancient buildings, marvel at the Crown Jewels, and stand in the very spots where pivotal historical events took place. Guided tours, exhibitions, and interactive displays provided an immersive experience, offering insight into the lives of kings, queens, and prisoners who once inhabited the Tower. This educational aspect of the Tower's tourism further enhanced its appeal as a cultural institution.

The Tower of London has become renowned for its spectacular exhibitions and displays that showcase its historical artifacts and treasures. The highlight for many visitors is the breathtaking display of the Crown Jewels, which includes magnificent crowns, scepters, and other regalia. These exhibits offer a rare glimpse into the opulence and grandeur of the British monarchy, captivating audiences and adding a touch of awe-inspiring splendor to the visitor experience.

To further engage visitors, the Tower of London has incorporated interactive experiences and living history performances. Skilled actors and interpreters bring the past to life, portraying historical characters and sharing captivating stories. Visitors can witness demonstrations of medieval weaponry, listen to tales of the Tower's infamous prisoners, and participate in interactive activities that allow them to step back in time. These immersive encounters create an engaging and memorable experience for visitors of all ages.

The opening of the Tower to the public has had a significant impact on the local economy. The influx of tourists has led to the growth of surrounding businesses, including hotels, restaurants, and souvenir shops. The Tower's popularity as a tourist destination has generated employment opportunities, benefiting the local community and contributing to the overall economic vitality of the area.

The revenue generated from tourism has played a crucial role in the preservation and conservation of the Tower of London. The funds generated through ticket sales and donations have supported ongoing maintenance, restoration projects, and the protection of the Tower's historic buildings and artifacts. This ensures that future generations can continue to explore and appreciate the Tower's rich heritage.

The Tower of London's opening to the public has transformed it into a world-renowned tourist destination, captivating visitors from near and far. Its historical significance, educational value, spectacular exhibitions, interactive experiences, and contribution to the local economy have made it a cultural institution that seamlessly combines the past and the present. The Tower's role in tourism not only allows visitors to explore England's fascinating history but also supports the preservation and conservation of this architectural marvel, ensuring that its legacy endures for generations to come.

The Tower of London, steeped in history and legends, has long been associated with reports of supernatural experiences and encounters. Visitors from around the world have shared chilling tales of ghostly apparitions, eerie sensations, and unexplained phenomena within the Tower's ancient walls. In this chapter, we delve into some of the reported supernatural experiences and encounters by visitors, adding to the mystique and intrigue that surrounds this iconic landmark.

One common supernatural encounter within the Tower is the sighting of ghostly apparitions of historical figures. Visitors have reported seeing spectral forms resembling Anne Boleyn, Lady Jane Grey, and other notable individuals who met tragic fates within the Tower. These ghostly apparitions are often described as translucent figures dressed in period clothing, adding an air of authenticity and historical resonance to the visitor's experience.

Numerous visitors have reported hearing disembodied whispers and phantom footsteps while exploring the Tower. These unexplained sounds often occur in empty corridors, echoing through the chambers and hallways. Some believe these auditory phenomena are the remnants of conversations and activities that occurred within the Tower's walls, forever etched into the fabric of its haunted history.

Many individuals who visit the Tower of London report experiencing feelings of unease, heaviness, or unexplained chills in certain areas. Cold spots, sudden drops in temperature, and atmospheric shifts have been reported, often associated with a sense of being watched or the presence of an unseen entity. These sensations contribute to the eerie ambiance of the Tower and evoke a heightened awareness of its haunted reputation.

Several visitors claim to have experienced unexplained touches or interactions with unseen forces while exploring the Tower. Some have reported feeling a light brush against their skin, as if someone or something unseen is attempting to make contact. Others claim to have had objects moved or knocked over, seemingly by an unseen hand. These encounters add an element of surprise and intrigue, leaving visitors contemplating the presence of supernatural forces within the Tower.

Psychics and sensitives who have visited the Tower of London have shared their impressions of the spiritual energy and emotional residue that lingers within its walls. They describe picking up on intense emotions, such as fear, sorrow, or anger, as if the events of the past continue to reverberate in the present. These psychic impressions offer glimpses into the deep emotional imprints left behind by those who suffered or met tragic fates within the Tower.

The Tower of London's reputation as a site of historical significance and paranormal activity has attracted visitors seeking encounters with the supernatural. Reports of ghostly apparitions, whispers, footsteps, unexplained touches, and psychic impressions contribute to the Tower's mystical allure. Whether these encounters are attributed to residual energy, the spirits of the past, or simply the power of suggestion, they add an extra layer of fascination and intrigue to the visitor experience. As individuals explore the Tower's ancient corridors and stand in the shadow of its historic structures, they cannot help but be drawn into the mysticism and haunted legacy that permeate this iconic landmark.

OLIVER LANCASTER

Chapter 15: The Ceremony of the Keys

———

The Tower of London is not only known for its historical importance and paranormal legends but also for its ceremonial traditions that have been upheld for centuries. Among these ceremonies, one of the most renowned is the Ceremony of the Keys, a nightly ritual that dates back to the medieval era. In this chapter, we explore the history and significance of this unique ceremony, delving into its origins, symbolism, and enduring legacy.

The origins of the Ceremony of the Keys can be traced back to the medieval period, although the exact date of its inception is uncertain. It is believed that the ceremony has been performed every night for over 700 years, making it one of the oldest ceremonial traditions in England. The ritual was established to safeguard the Tower and its precious contents, ensuring its security and protection from external threats.

The Ceremony of the Keys symbolizes the importance of safeguarding the Tower and its historical treasures. The ritual is a symbolic act of handing over the responsibility for the Tower's security from the military guard to the Yeoman Warder, who represents the monarch. The ceremony signifies the unbroken continuity of this duty, emphasizing the Tower's significance as a stronghold of power and the protection of the realm.

The ceremony takes place every night at exactly 9:53 PM. The Chief Yeoman Warder, accompanied by a small escort of guards carrying lanterns and keys, proceeds to the Byward Tower. At the outer gate of the Tower, known as the Middle Tower, they are met by a sentry from the military guard. The Chief Yeoman Warder then declares, "Halt, who comes there?" and the sentry responds, "The keys." The exchange continues as the ceremonial guard escorts the Chief Yeoman Warder to the Bloody Tower, where the keys are handed over and the gates are locked for the night.

The Ceremony of the Keys is shrouded in secrecy and conducted with meticulous precision. The strict adherence to the ceremonial protocol and the solemn atmosphere contribute to the sense of tradition and the preservation of the Tower's historical legacy. The ceremony has withstood the test of time, remaining largely unchanged throughout the centuries, symbolizing the enduring traditions and values associated with the Tower.

While the Ceremony of the Keys is a long-standing tradition, it is also a highly coveted event for visitors to witness. A limited number of people are allowed to attend each night, and tickets must be requested well in advance due to the high demand. The public's interest in the ceremony reflects its significance as a symbol of national heritage and the enduring appeal of ancient traditions.

The Ceremony of the Keys at the Tower of London represents a unique blend of history, symbolism, and tradition. This nightly ritual, steeped in secrecy and conducted with precision, embodies the responsibility and honor of safeguarding the Tower and its storied past. The ceremony's longevity and continued public interest demonstrate its enduring significance, allowing visitors to connect with the Tower's rich heritage and witness a centuries-old tradition that echoes through the annals of time.

The Ceremony of the Keys, a time-honored tradition at the Tower of London, is not only steeped in history and symbolism but has also been associated with paranormal occurrences and ghostly sightings. As the night unfolds and the ritual unfolds, visitors and participants have reported eerie experiences, mysterious phenomena, and spectral apparitions that add an extra layer of intrigue to this already captivating ceremony. In this chapter, we delve into some of the paranormal occurrences and ghostly sightings that have been attributed to the Ceremony of the Keys.

During the Ceremony of the Keys, participants and witnesses have reported hearing unexplained footsteps and whispers. These phantom sounds, often described as echoing through the ancient corridors and chambers of the Tower, create an atmosphere of unease and mystery. Some believe these auditory phenomena are the residual echoes of the past, as if the spirits of long-departed guardians and figures associated with the Tower still haunt its hallowed halls.

The solemnity and historical significance of the Ceremony of the Keys have led to reports of spectral figures seen during the ritual. Witnesses claim to have glimpsed ghostly apparitions of historical figures associated with the Tower, such as Anne

Boleyn, Lady Jane Grey, or other notable individuals who met tragic ends within its walls. These ethereal manifestations, often described as translucent or glowing figures, seem to momentarily appear and disappear, leaving an indelible impression on those who bear witness.

Some participants in the Ceremony of the Keys have experienced sudden drops in temperature and encountered inexplicable cold spots. These chilling areas are often attributed to the presence of supernatural energy or the passing of spirits. Visitors have described feeling a distinct change in the air, as if an unseen presence has enveloped them, heightening their awareness of the paranormal forces that intertwine with the ceremony.

Individuals who take part in the Ceremony of the Keys have reported eerie sensations and unexplained touches. Some have described feeling a gentle brush against their skin or the sensation of being watched, even when there is no visible presence nearby. These encounters contribute to a sense of the otherworldly and suggest that the spirits connected to the Tower are aware of the ceremony and continue to interact with those involved.

Psychics and sensitives who have attended the Ceremony of the Keys claim to have picked up on psychic impressions and emotional residue associated with the Tower's history. They describe feeling overwhelming emotions, such as fear, sadness, or anxiety, as if tapping into the residual energy left behind by the tumultuous events that unfolded within the Tower's walls. These impressions serve as a haunting reminder of the profound impact that history and tragedy have had on the spiritual realm of the Tower.

The Ceremony of the Keys, a revered tradition at the Tower of London, has been intertwined with reports of paranormal occurrences and ghostly sightings. Witnesses have encountered phantom footsteps, whispers, apparitions of historical figures, temperature fluctuations, unexplained touches, and psychic impressions during the ritual. These paranormal experiences add an extra layer of intrigue and fascination to the already captivating atmosphere surrounding the ceremony. Whether they are attributed to residual energy, the spirits of the departed, or the power of suggestion, these encounters leave an indelible mark on those who participate in or witness the Ceremony of the Keys, perpetuating the mystique and haunted reputation of the Tower of London.

OLIVER LANCASTER

Chapter 16: The Legend of the Two Princes

─────

The fate of the Princes in the Tower, Edward V and Richard of Shrewsbury, has remained one of the most enduring mysteries in English history. Their disappearance and presumed deaths have fueled centuries of speculation, leading to various suspects and theories regarding their fate. In this chapter, we delve into the possible suspects and explore the theories that have emerged over the years, shedding light on this perplexing historical enigma.

One of the most widely debated suspects in the fate of the Princes is Richard III, who assumed the throne following their disappearance. According to some theories, Richard III ordered their murder in order to secure his own claim to the crown. This theory gained traction due to Richard III's troubled reign and the discovery of the Princes' remains in the Tower in the 17th century. However, others argue that Richard III may have been wrongly accused, and his involvement in the Princes' fate remains a matter of speculation.

Henry VII, the first Tudor king, is another possible suspect in the disappearance of the Princes. Some theories suggest that Henry VII had the Princes killed to eliminate potential rivals to his throne. The timing of the disappearance, which coincided with Henry VII's ascent to power, has fueled suspicions. However, like the Richard III theory, concrete evidence linking Henry VII to the Princes' fate is lacking, leaving room for ongoing speculation and debate.

Margaret Beaufort, Henry VII's mother, and the Tudor faction have also been implicated in the fate of the Princes. The theory suggests that Margaret Beaufort and her allies orchestrated the murder of the Princes to ensure Henry VII's claim to the throne. Their involvement is often viewed as a politically motivated act to consolidate power. However, like the other theories, there is a lack of conclusive evidence to substantiate these claims.

Beyond Richard III and the Tudor faction, several other individuals have been proposed as possible suspects in the Princes' fate. These include various members of the nobility, such as the Duke of Buckingham, who may have had their own motivations for eliminating the Princes. Additionally, some theories suggest that the Princes' fate may have been the result of a plot involving multiple individuals rather than a single perpetrator. The lack of definitive evidence has allowed for a range of suspects and theories to emerge, adding to the enduring mystery surrounding the Princes in the Tower.

In addition to specific suspects, alternative theories have been proposed to explain the fate of the Princes. These include the possibility that they were smuggled out of the Tower and lived in secret, or that they died from natural causes or accidents. Some theories even suggest that the remains found in the Tower were not those of the Princes, raising questions about their true fate and the potential for their survival.

THE TOWER OF LONDON: THE HAUNTED PAST AND SECRETS OF ROYAL GHOSTS

The fate of the Princes in the Tower remains a captivating historical mystery that has fascinated scholars and enthusiasts for centuries. Richard III, Henry VII, Margaret Beaufort, and other individuals have been named as possible suspects in their disappearance, each with their own motivations and theories. However, the lack of concrete evidence and the passage of time have made it challenging to uncover the truth behind this enigma. As the centuries pass, the fate of the Princes in the Tower continues to intrigue, leaving historians and sleuths alike to grapple with unanswered questions and engage in ongoing speculation.

The disappearance and presumed deaths of the Princes in the Tower, Edward V and Richard of Shrewsbury, have not only left a historical mystery but have also given rise to legends and reports of ghostly encounters. The tragic fate of these young royal figures has become intertwined with spectral tales and haunting experiences within the Tower of London. In this chapter, we delve into the reported ghostly encounters and legends associated with the Princes in the Tower, adding a chilling dimension to their enigmatic story.

Visitors, staff, and even residents of the Tower have reported sightings of ghostly childlike figures believed to be the spirits of the Princes in the Tower. These apparitions are often described as young boys dressed in period clothing, their faces filled with sadness and a sense of longing. Witnesses claim to have glimpsed these ethereal figures wandering the Tower's corridors or appearing near their alleged place of confinement, leaving an indelible impression on those who encounter them.

Whispers and cries echoing through the Tower's walls have been attributed to the restless spirits of the Princes. Visitors and caretakers have reported hearing disembodied voices, often in the vicinity of the rooms where the Princes were believed to have been held captive. These spectral sounds, filled with sorrow and anguish, evoke a sense of their tragic fate and perpetuate the belief that the spirits of the young Princes continue to haunt the Tower.

Cold spots and chilling sensations have been associated with the presence of the Princes' spirits. Visitors to specific areas of the Tower linked to their alleged confinement have reported sudden drops in temperature, even in the absence of any logical explanation. Some have described feeling an icy touch or a presence that sends shivers down their spines, as if the spirits of the Princes make their presence felt through these chilling sensations.

Unexplained movements and disturbances of objects have been attributed to the Princes' spirits within the Tower. Caretakers and witnesses claim that items are mysteriously displaced or knocked over, seemingly without any rational cause. While some skeptics may dismiss these incidents as mere coincidences, believers interpret them as signs of the Princes' presence, as if they attempt to communicate with the living through these subtle acts.

Psychics and sensitives who have visited the Tower have reported picking up on psychic impressions and emotional residue associated with the Princes. They describe feeling overwhelmed by feelings of fear, sadness, and despair, as if tapping into the lingering energy left behind by the Princes' tragic fate. These impressions serve as a haunting reminder of the profound impact that their untimely demise had on the spiritual realm of the Tower.

The legend of the Princes in the Tower, forever linked to their mysterious disappearance and presumed deaths, has sparked reports of ghostly encounters and spectral phenomena within the Tower of London. Apparitions of childlike figures, whispers, cries in the night, cold spots, mysterious object movements, and psychic impressions all contribute to the eerie aura surrounding the Princes' story. Whether these encounters are attributed to the restless spirits of the Princes or the power of suggestion, they add an extra layer of intrigue to their enigmatic tale, perpetuating the belief that their presence lingers within the haunted confines of the Tower.

OLIVER LANCASTER

Chapter 17: The Haunted Tower Bridge

Tower Bridge, an iconic symbol of London, has not only witnessed historical events but has also been associated with reports of supernatural experiences and hauntings. The bridge's majestic architecture and rich history have contributed to the belief that lingering spirits and ghostly phenomena inhabit its structure. In this chapter, we explore the reported supernatural experiences and hauntings associated with Tower Bridge, adding a chilling dimension to its already captivating allure.

One of the most frequently reported apparitions associated with Tower Bridge is that of the Lady in White. Witnesses claim to have seen a spectral figure, often described as a young woman in flowing white clothing, walking along the walkways or peering out from the bridge's towers. The identity of the Lady in White remains unknown, but her presence is believed to be linked to tragic events or unsettled spirits tied to the bridge's history.

Numerous accounts mention sightings of ghostly figures resembling workers and engineers from the bridge's construction era. These apparitions are often described as transparent or ethereal forms engaged in their tasks, as if reliving their duties from the past. Witnesses have reported seeing these spectral workers on the catwalks, operating machinery, or inspecting the bridge's structure. Their presence adds an otherworldly dimension to the bridge's history and construction.

Visitors and workers on Tower Bridge have reported unexplained auditory phenomena. These include hearing footsteps, voices, or the sounds of tools and machinery, even when no one is present. Some witnesses claim to hear distant conversations or murmurs as if the bridge's invisible occupants continue their activities from long ago. These spectral sounds contribute to the bridge's haunting ambiance and evoke a sense of its bustling history.

Many individuals who have crossed or spent time on Tower Bridge describe experiencing an eerie atmosphere and unsettling sensations. Some report feelings of being watched, a heaviness in the air, or a sense of unease that cannot be attributed to any logical cause. These sensations are often associated with the presence of spirits or residual energy connected to the bridge's past, heightening the bridge's enigmatic allure.

A few accounts suggest that individuals have experienced time slips or encountered anachronistic scenes while on Tower Bridge. Witnesses claim to have briefly glimpsed scenes from different time periods, seeing people dressed in old-fashioned attire or witnessing events that appeared to be from the bridge's historical past. These experiences, if true, suggest a temporal overlap between the present and the bridge's bygone eras, adding an element of temporal distortion to its supernatural reputation.

THE TOWER OF LONDON: THE HAUNTED PAST AND SECRETS OF ROYAL GHOSTS

Tower Bridge, with its imposing structure and historical significance, has fostered reports of supernatural experiences and hauntings. The apparitions of the Lady in White, phantom workers, auditory phenomena, eerie atmospheres, and anachronistic encounters contribute to the bridge's mystique and add a chilling dimension to its allure. Whether these encounters are attributed to residual energy, the spirits of the departed, or the power of suggestion, they leave an indelible mark on those who have experienced them, perpetuating the bridge's reputation as a site of paranormal activity. As visitors cross Tower Bridge, they cannot help but wonder if the spirits of the past continue to reside within its majestic towers and walkways, forever intertwined with the bridge's timeless legacy.

While Tower Bridge is widely recognized for its iconic towers and magnificent bascule bridge, there is a hidden and enigmatic space beneath its surface—the Tower Bridge Engine Room. Serving as the operational heart of the bridge, this intriguing chamber holds its own share of secrets and mysteries. In this chapter, we delve into the history and explore the reported supernatural experiences and intriguing phenomena associated with the Tower Bridge Engine Room.

The Tower Bridge Engine Room was built in the late 19th century to house the machinery responsible for raising and lowering the bridge. Steam-powered engines, hydraulic systems, and intricate mechanisms were housed within this space, allowing for the controlled movement of the bridge's massive bascules. The Engine Room served as a testament to Victorian engineering prowess and provided a glimpse into the technological advancements of the time.

Over the years, several visitors and workers in the Tower Bridge Engine Room have reported supernatural encounters and eerie phenomena. Some claim to have witnessed unexplained apparitions or heard disembodied voices echoing through the chamber. Shadows flitting across the walls, unexplained movements of machinery, and sudden changes in temperature have also been reported, leaving many to ponder the existence of paranormal activity within the Engine Room.

One particular legend associated with the Tower Bridge Engine Room involves the ghostly presence of an engineer who tragically lost his life during the bridge's construction. According to the story, his spirit is said to roam the Engine Room, eternally connected to the mechanisms he once operated. Visitors and workers have claimed to catch glimpses of a figure in engineering attire, sensing his watchful presence or even hearing the sound of his footsteps.

There have been reports of electromagnetic anomalies within the Tower Bridge Engine Room. Visitors and paranormal investigators have documented unusual fluctuations in electromagnetic fields, which some believe could be a potential indicator of paranormal energy. These anomalies, coupled with the reported ghostly encounters, have contributed to the intrigue surrounding the Engine Room's supernatural reputation.

Psychics and sensitives who have visited the Tower Bridge Engine Room have described picking up on psychic impressions and residual energy within the space. They have reported sensing the presence of past workers, the emotions connected to the construction and operation of the bridge, and the lingering energy left behind by the powerful machinery. These impressions offer a glimpse into the history and human connections that continue to resonate within the Engine Room.

The Tower Bridge Engine Room, though no longer in active use, serves as a testament to the bridge's engineering marvels and historical significance. While the reported supernatural experiences and mysteries associated with the Engine Room add an intriguing layer to its story, it is crucial to preserve and protect this space as an essential part of Tower Bridge's heritage. By acknowledging and exploring its supernatural reputation, the Engine Room continues to captivate visitors and enthusiasts, leaving them with a deeper appreciation for its hidden wonders.

The Tower Bridge Engine Room, with its history, technological marvels, and reported supernatural experiences, remains an enigmatic space within the iconic bridge. Ghostly encounters, electromagnetic anomalies, the haunting tale of the engineer, psychic impressions, and energy residue intertwine to create a sense of mystery and fascination. As visitors venture into the depths of the Engine Room, they cannot help but contemplate the bridge's hidden dimensions, where the echoes of the past and the possibility of the paranormal converge in a captivating blend of history and the supernatural.

OLIVER LANCASTER

Chapter 18: The Tower's Restoration and Preservation

The Tower of London, with its rich history and architectural significance, requires ongoing efforts to ensure its preservation for future generations. Over the years, various restoration projects have been undertaken to safeguard the Tower's structural integrity, protect its historic fabric, and maintain its cultural significance. In this chapter, we explore the restoration efforts made and their impact on the site's history.

Restoration plays a crucial role in maintaining the Tower of London as a living historical monument. The aging infrastructure, exposure to the elements, and the wear and tear of centuries necessitate continuous maintenance and conservation work. Restoration projects are vital not only for preserving the physical fabric of the Tower but also for safeguarding its historical and cultural value, allowing visitors to experience its grandeur and significance.

Restoration efforts at the Tower of London are guided by a conservation philosophy that emphasizes retaining as much of the original fabric as possible. The aim is to ensure that any interventions are respectful, reversible, and based on meticulous research and analysis. This approach allows the Tower to retain its authenticity and integrity, preserving the layers of history embedded within its walls.

Major Restoration Projects:

Several significant restoration projects have been undertaken at the Tower of London, each leaving a lasting impact on the site's history.

1. The White Tower: The restoration of the White Tower, the oldest and most iconic structure within the complex, was a milestone project. The restoration work included repairs to the exterior stonework, roof, windows, and interiors. This project not only enhanced the structural stability of the tower but also improved the visitor experience by providing access to previously inaccessible areas and creating informative displays.

2. The Chapel Royal of St. Peter ad Vincula: This historic chapel, where many notable figures, including Anne Boleyn and Lady Jane Grey, are buried, underwent restoration to preserve its architectural features and repair any damage. The project focused on preserving the intricate stone carvings, stained glass windows, and the overall integrity of the chapel, ensuring its historical and spiritual significance remains intact.

3. The Crown Jewels: The restoration and preservation of the Crown Jewels are of utmost importance to protect these national treasures. The display areas were upgraded, ensuring optimal security, lighting, and climate control to safeguard the jewels' condition and enhance their presentation. This project aimed to provide visitors with an immersive and awe-inspiring experience while ensuring the long-term preservation of these priceless artifacts.

Impact on the Site's History:

THE TOWER OF LONDON: THE HAUNTED PAST AND SECRETS OF ROYAL GHOSTS

The restoration efforts at the Tower of London have had a profound impact on the site's history. Through meticulous research, analysis, and careful restoration, these projects have uncovered hidden details, revived architectural elements, and shed new light on the Tower's past. The restoration work ensures that the site remains a living testament to the diverse layers of history it encompasses, allowing visitors to appreciate and engage with its rich heritage.

Preserving the Tower's Legacy:

The restoration and preservation of the Tower of London are ongoing endeavors. Continued monitoring, maintenance, and conservation practices are essential to mitigate the impact of time, environmental factors, and visitor traffic on the site. By investing in restoration projects, the Tower's legacy is preserved, ensuring that its historical, architectural, and cultural significance endures for generations to come.

The restoration and preservation of the Tower of London are fundamental to safeguarding its historical integrity and cultural value. Through major restoration projects and the application of conservation principles, the Tower's structures, artifacts, and stories are meticulously preserved and presented to visitors. These efforts not only maintain the site's physical condition but also allow future generations to experience the grandeur, learn from the past, and appreciate the Tower of London as a living historical monument.

Restoration and preservation activities at the Tower of London, while essential for maintaining its historical integrity, have also been accompanied by reports of paranormal experiences. The combination of delicate work on ancient structures, the uncovering of hidden spaces, and the reverence for the site's history has created an environment that some believe to be conducive to supernatural encounters. In this chapter, we highlight the paranormal experiences reported by those involved in restoration and preservation activities at the Tower of London.

During restoration projects, workers and preservation teams have reported hearing unexplained noises and footsteps within the Tower's walls. These auditory phenomena often occur when the areas being worked on are believed to be empty. Some workers have described hearing faint conversations, whispers, or the sound of footsteps echoing through deserted corridors. These mysterious sounds add an eerie ambiance to the restoration process, suggesting the presence of unseen entities connected to the Tower's history.

Numerous individuals engaged in restoration and preservation work at the Tower have reported sightings of apparitions or ghostly figures. Some have claimed to witness translucent forms dressed in period clothing, resembling historical figures associated with the Tower's past. These sightings often occur in dimly lit areas or secluded sections of the complex, leaving workers with an unnerving sense that they are not alone. The apparitions are believed to be the spirits of those who once lived or worked within the Tower's walls.

Temperature fluctuations and cold spots are commonly reported during restoration and preservation activities at the

THE TOWER OF LONDON: THE HAUNTED PAST AND SECRETS OF ROYAL GHOSTS

Tower of London. Workers have experienced sudden drops in temperature, even in spaces that should be well insulated. These cold spots, sometimes accompanied by feelings of being watched or a sense of unease, are often interpreted as signs of supernatural presence. Some believe that these fluctuations reflect the energy of the spirits connected to the Tower, manifesting in tangible ways during restoration work.

During restoration projects, workers have encountered unexplained equipment malfunctions that defy rational explanation. Tools and machinery have been known to malfunction or cease functioning altogether, only to resume normal operation once workers move away from certain areas or complete their work. These incidents, often attributed to paranormal interference, add an extra layer of mystery and frustration to the restoration process.

Some individuals with psychic abilities or heightened sensitivity have participated in restoration and preservation activities at the Tower of London. These individuals have reported picking up on psychic impressions, emotional residue, or energetic imprints left by the Tower's past inhabitants. They describe feeling overwhelming emotions, such as sadness, fear, or excitement, as they connect with the historical energies embedded within the structures. These psychic impressions provide a unique insight into the layers of history being uncovered during restoration work.

The restoration and preservation of the Tower of London, while vital for its continued existence, have been accompanied by reports of paranormal experiences. Unexplained noises, sightings of apparitions, temperature fluctuations, equipment malfunctions, and psychic impressions are just some of the phenomena encountered by those involved in restoration and preservation activities. These experiences highlight the profound connection between the Tower's history, the delicate work being undertaken, and the ethereal presence of the past. Whether attributed to residual energy, the spirits of the departed, or the power of suggestion, these paranormal encounters add an extra layer of intrigue and fascination to the restoration process, perpetuating the Tower of London's reputation as a site of supernatural activity.

THE TOWER OF LONDON: THE HAUNTED PAST AND SECRETS OF ROYAL GHOSTS

Chapter 19: Famous Visitors and Their Encounters

———

The Tower of London, with its rich history and haunted reputation, has attracted the attention of numerous notable figures throughout the years. Many of these individuals have reported paranormal encounters and eerie experiences while visiting or residing within the Tower's walls. In this chapter, we delve into the accounts of paranormal encounters by notable figures, shedding light on their personal experiences and the impact it had on their perceptions of the Tower.

Sir Walter Raleigh, the famed explorer and poet, was imprisoned in the Tower of London on multiple occasions. During his confinement, Raleigh reportedly encountered ghostly apparitions within his cell. He claimed to have seen the specter of Anne Boleyn, the ill-fated queen, walking the corridors of the Tower. Raleigh's account of this encounter contributes to the belief that the spirits of historical figures continue to haunt the Tower's confines.

Captain Markham, a former governor of the Tower, also had a chilling encounter with the supernatural. While residing in the Queen's House, he claimed to have seen the ghostly figure of a woman dressed in white, known as the Lady in White. This spectral apparition was believed to be the spirit of a former resident or a tragic figure associated with the Tower's past.

Captain Markham's account adds credibility to the enduring legend of the Lady in White.

Dame Sybil Penn, the daughter of a prominent nobleman, spent time at the Tower of London during the Tudor period. She reported witnessing supernatural phenomena, including disembodied voices, unexplained footsteps, and objects moving on their own accord. These eerie experiences left a lasting impact on Dame Sybil Penn, leading her to believe in the presence of restless spirits within the Tower's walls.

John Stow, a renowned historian and chronicler of London's history, recorded several paranormal encounters within the Tower of London. He described hearing cries and screams during the night, particularly in the vicinity of the Beauchamp Tower, which was known for its grim history of imprisonment and torture. Stow's accounts provide valuable historical documentation of the paranormal activity associated with the Tower.

Even in medieval times, notable figures experienced supernatural encounters at the Tower of London. Thomas Becket, the Archbishop of Canterbury, claimed to have heard celestial music and voices while imprisoned in the Tower in the 12th century. These divine manifestations were interpreted as signs of his sanctity and eventual martyrdom. Becket's experiences highlight the enduring belief in divine intervention and the presence of the spiritual realm within the Tower's confines.

THE TOWER OF LONDON: THE HAUNTED PAST AND SECRETS OF ROYAL GHOSTS

Notable figures throughout history have encountered the paranormal within the Tower of London, contributing to its haunted reputation. Sir Walter Raleigh, Captain Markham, Dame Sybil Penn, John Stow, and Thomas Becket are just a few of the individuals who reported ghostly encounters, unexplained phenomena, and eerie experiences within the Tower's walls. Their accounts add credibility to the enduring legends and folklore associated with the Tower, perpetuating the belief in its supernatural inhabitants. Whether attributed to the restless spirits of historical figures or the residual energy of traumatic events, these encounters leave an indelible mark on those who experience them, solidifying the Tower of London's position as one of the most haunted locations in the world.

The Tower of London's reputation as one of the most haunted places in the world has been shaped by the numerous accounts of paranormal encounters and eerie experiences reported by visitors, residents, and notable figures throughout history. These encounters have had a profound impact on the Tower's reputation, solidifying its position as a site imbued with supernatural energy and intrigue. In this chapter, we explore the influence of these encounters on the Tower's reputation and its enduring status as a haunted landmark.

The paranormal encounters and eerie experiences reported at the Tower of London have played a significant role in amplifying its mystique and allure. Stories of ghostly apparitions, unexplained noises, and chilling sensations have perpetuated the belief that the Tower is a place where the boundaries between the living and the dead blur. The accounts of notable figures and their encounters add credibility to the legends and folklore associated with the Tower, contributing to its reputation as a site of paranormal activity.

The paranormal encounters within the Tower of London have also enhanced its historical narrative. Many of these encounters are connected to significant historical figures, such as Anne Boleyn or Thomas Becket, adding another layer of depth to their stories and the events that unfolded within the Tower's walls. The accounts of notable figures who experienced the supernatural firsthand have become part of the Tower's historical tapestry, intertwining the realms of fact and folklore and enriching the understanding of its past.

The Tower's reputation as a haunted landmark has undoubtedly played a role in attracting visitors from around the world. The allure of encountering the supernatural, walking in the footsteps of historical figures, and exploring the Tower's mysterious atmosphere has drawn countless curious individuals seeking a glimpse into its haunted history. The reported paranormal encounters act as a magnet for those interested in the occult, history, and the enigmatic nature of the Tower, contributing to its continued popularity as a tourist destination.

The paranormal encounters at the Tower of London have perpetuated its legacy as a site steeped in history, tragedy, and the supernatural. The accounts passed down through generations, including those of notable figures, ensure that the stories of the Tower's hauntings remain ingrained in its cultural fabric. The tales of ghostly encounters continue to captivate the imagination and spark intrigue, allowing the Tower's reputation as a haunted place to endure over time.

The Tower's reputation for paranormal activity has also inspired numerous works of literature, films, and other media. From Gothic novels to historical dramas, the Tower's haunted reputation has served as a backdrop for captivating stories that explore the intertwining realms of history and the supernatural. The reported encounters by notable figures have provided fodder for these creative endeavors, further perpetuating the Tower's reputation as a site of eerie encounters and ghostly phenomena.

The accounts of paranormal encounters at the Tower of London have had a profound impact on its reputation and legacy. These encounters, reported by notable figures and others who have experienced the supernatural within the Tower's walls, have amplified its mystique, enhanced its historical narrative, attracted curious visitors, perpetuated its legacy, and inspired works of literature and media. The Tower's haunted reputation continues to thrive, captivating the imagination and ensuring that its connection to the supernatural remains an integral part of its enduring allure.

OLIVER LANCASTER

Chapter 20: The Enduring Mysteries of the Tower

———

The Tower of London stands as an enduring symbol of British history, a fortress steeped in centuries of political intrigue, royal drama, and haunting tales. Its historical significance and enduring fascination lie in its multifaceted roles as a royal palace, a fortress, a prison, and a repository of priceless treasures. In this chapter, we reflect on the Tower's historical importance and the reasons behind its enduring fascination.

Throughout its long history, the Tower of London has borne witness to pivotal moments that shaped the course of British history. From its construction in the 11th century to its role as a royal residence and a site of imprisonment, the Tower has been entwined with the lives of monarchs, nobles, and political figures. It has seen coronations, executions, and acts of rebellion, offering a tangible link to the triumphs and tragedies that have defined the nation's past.

The Tower's towering presence and formidable architecture have long symbolized the power and authority of the British monarchy. As a royal fortress and residence, it served as a visual reminder of the Crown's strength and influence. The Tower's role in safeguarding the Crown Jewels, the coronation regalia, and other treasures reinforced its significance as a repository of national heritage and a symbol of royal authority.

The Tower's iconic architecture, including the imposing White Tower and the picturesque turrets and battlements, has captivated visitors for centuries. Its distinctive silhouette against the London skyline and its historic buildings, such as the Chapel Royal of St. Peter ad Vincula and the Bloody Tower, have become instantly recognizable symbols of London and British history. The Tower's architectural grandeur, combined with its rich historical associations, has contributed to its enduring fascination.

The Tower of London's association with royal intrigue and tragedy has fueled its enduring fascination. Stories of monarchs like Henry VIII and his six wives, the mysterious disappearance of the Princes in the Tower, and the execution of Anne Boleyn have become embedded in the Tower's lore. The tales of political machinations, betrayal, and dramatic events have transformed the Tower into a repository of historical mysteries, captivating the imaginations of both historians and the general public.

The Tower's reputation as one of the most haunted places in the world has added to its allure. Reports of ghostly encounters, paranormal phenomena, and the legends surrounding figures like the Lady in White and Anne Boleyn's ghost have created an air of mystery and intrigue. The Tower's haunted history evokes a sense of the past merging with the present, allowing visitors to connect with the spirits of history and experience the uncanny within its ancient walls.

The continuous efforts to preserve and protect the Tower of London highlight its enduring cultural significance.

THE TOWER OF LONDON: THE HAUNTED PAST AND SECRETS OF ROYAL GHOSTS

Restoration projects, conservation practices, and the careful management of its historical artifacts and structures ensure that the Tower's legacy is safeguarded for future generations. Its status as a UNESCO World Heritage site underscores its global importance as a living historical monument.

The Tower of London's historical significance and enduring fascination stem from its multifaceted roles as a witness to history, a symbol of power, an iconic architectural masterpiece, and a repository of tales of royal intrigue and tragedy. Its haunted reputation and cultural significance have further contributed to its allure. As visitors walk within its ancient walls, they become part of a continuum that spans centuries, connecting with the triumphs, tragedies, and enigmatic stories that define the Tower's enduring place in British history and its indelible mark on the world's imagination.

As we conclude this exploration of the Tower of London's haunted past and enduring fascination, it is important to remember that the stories, legends, and encounters recounted throughout this book are but a glimpse into the enigmatic realm of the Tower's history. The Tower of London invites you to embark on your own journey of discovery and form your own conclusions about its haunted past.

Venture within its ancient walls, wander through its historic chambers, and let your imagination transport you to a time when monarchs ruled, prisoners languished, and spirits may still roam. Listen to the whispers of history carried on the wind, immerse yourself in the chilling atmosphere, and allow the Tower to reveal its secrets in its own time.

Whether you are a history enthusiast, a believer in the supernatural, or simply intrigued by the mysteries of the past, the Tower of London offers an unparalleled opportunity to explore the convergence of history and haunting. Engage with the Tower's rich tapestry of stories, from the tragic fate of Anne Boleyn to the mysterious disappearance of the Princes in the Tower. Stand in awe before the Crown Jewels and contemplate the weight of their hidden histories. Feel the echoes of past footsteps as you traverse the very same paths walked by kings, queens, and prisoners.

But above all, embrace the spirit of discovery and form your own conclusions. Allow the Tower's haunted past to unfold before you, leaving room for wonder, skepticism, or a mix of both. Engage with the tales of paranormal encounters, weigh the historical evidence, and let your experiences within the Tower shape your perspective.

For the Tower of London is not merely a relic frozen in time; it is a living monument that invites us to connect with the spirits of the past, to question our understanding of history, and to embrace the unknown. It is a place where fact and legend intertwine, where the ethereal and the tangible converge, and where the boundaries between the realms of the living and the dead blur.

So, step through the gates of the Tower of London with an open mind and a sense of adventure. Let its haunted past envelop you, allowing the stories of centuries to whisper in your ear. In this realm of intrigue and spectral mysteries, you may find yourself forming your own conclusions, unlocking new insights, and discovering the haunting allure of one of the world's most iconic landmarks.

Conclusion

The Tower of London's haunted reputation and its connection to royal ghosts have contributed to its enduring fascination and allure. Throughout its long history, the Tower has become synonymous with tales of paranormal encounters, ghostly apparitions, and unexplained phenomena. From the spectral figure of Anne Boleyn to the Lady in White and other restless spirits, the Tower is believed to house the ethereal remnants of the past.

These ghostly encounters and legends have woven a tapestry of haunted history, intertwining the supernatural with the tangible realm of royalty and power. The Tower's association with tragic events, political intrigue, and the imprisonment and execution of historical figures has created an atmosphere charged with spectral energy.

Visitors, residents, and notable figures alike have reported chilling experiences, from hearing phantom footsteps and cries echoing through the corridors to catching glimpses of ghostly apparitions. These encounters have left an indelible mark on the Tower's reputation, solidifying its position as one of the most haunted locations in the world.

The connection to royal ghosts adds a layer of mystique and fascination to the Tower's haunted reputation. As the abode of kings and queens throughout history, it is believed that the spirits of these monarchs and their ill-fated consorts continue to wander the Tower's halls, perpetuating their stories and imprinting their presence on the fabric of the site.

While skeptics may question the existence of these ghostly inhabitants, the Tower of London's haunted reputation endures, captivating the imagination of visitors from all walks of life. The allure lies in the possibility of encountering the supernatural, stepping into the world of the past, and experiencing the enigmatic intersection of history and the ethereal.

So, as you embark on your own exploration of the Tower of London, immerse yourself in its haunted reputation. Allow the legends and encounters to ignite your curiosity and spark your imagination. Be open to the whispers of the past and the possibility of encountering royal ghosts as you delve into the Tower's rich tapestry of history and haunting.

But remember, it is ultimately for you to decide the truth behind the Tower's haunted reputation. Form your own conclusions, draw inspiration from the accounts and legends, and let your own experiences shape your understanding of the Tower's spectral realm.

Whether you believe in the supernatural or approach it with skepticism, the Tower of London's haunted reputation invites you to explore its mysteries, immerse yourself in its history, and embark on a journey where the boundaries between the living and the dead become blurred.

Throughout this book, we have delved into the intriguing stories and legends surrounding the Tower of London. From its haunted past to the secrets of royal ghosts, each chapter has uncovered layers of history, mystery, and the supernatural. As we reflect on the stories and legends explored, we are reminded of the captivating power of folklore and the enduring fascination with the Tower's enigmatic allure.

The tales of Anne Boleyn's ghost, the Lady in White, and the Princes in the Tower have left an indelible mark on the Tower's reputation. These stories, passed down through generations, have become intertwined with its history, blurring the line between fact and fiction. They remind us of the enduring power of storytelling, as we continue to be captivated by the mysteries that surround these spectral figures.

The Tower's role as a fortress, a royal residence, and a place of imprisonment has provided a backdrop for dramatic events and tragic fates. The execution of notable figures such as Anne Boleyn and the imprisonment of Sir Walter Raleigh have become embedded in the Tower's narrative, perpetuating its haunted reputation. These stories remind us of the human drama and the emotional weight carried by the Tower's stone walls.

The architecture of the Tower itself, from the White Tower to the Chapel Royal, has added to its allure. Its iconic features, such as the Traitor's Gate and the Bloody Tower, have become symbols of the Tower's history and have inspired tales of paranormal encounters. These stories remind us of the impact that physical spaces can have on our perception of the supernatural and the power of the imagination.

The restoration and preservation efforts at the Tower have highlighted the importance of safeguarding its historical fabric. Through these projects, we ensure that the stories and legends of the Tower continue to be preserved and cherished. The paranormal encounters reported during these endeavors remind us that the past is not just a distant memory, but an ever-present presence that can be felt and experienced.

As we reflect on the stories and legends explored throughout this book, we are reminded of the timeless appeal of the Tower of London. Its haunted reputation, intertwined with history and folklore, continues to captivate the imagination of visitors and enthusiasts from around the world. These stories serve as a testament to the enduring power of the Tower's mysteries and the unending fascination with its haunted past.

In the end, it is up to each reader to navigate the realm of history and the supernatural, to question, to ponder, and to form their own conclusions. The Tower of London invites us to embrace the allure of its stories and legends, to step into its haunted realm, and to explore the rich tapestry of its enigmatic past.

As we conclude this journey through the stories, legends, and mysteries of the Tower of London, we invite you to answer the call of this remarkable fortress and embark on your own adventure within its ancient walls. For no words on a page can truly capture the essence of the Tower's rich history and supernatural allure. It beckons you to experience it firsthand, to immerse yourself in its captivating atmosphere, and to uncover its hidden secrets.

THE TOWER OF LONDON: THE HAUNTED PAST AND SECRETS OF ROYAL GHOSTS

Visiting the Tower of London is an opportunity to step back in time and walk in the footsteps of kings, queens, and prisoners. As you explore its historic chambers, winding corridors, and formidable towers, you will feel the weight of centuries of history bearing down upon you. The tangible presence of the past, intertwined with the ethereal realm of the supernatural, will envelop you.

Listen closely as you venture through the Tower's confines. Let the echoes of the past whisper in your ear, sharing tales of triumphs, tragedies, and the haunting legends that have made the Tower infamous. Pay a visit to the Chapel Royal of St. Peter ad Vincula, where the remains of the executed lie in rest, and let the solemnity of the space transport you to another time.

Marvel at the Crown Jewels, beholding the breathtaking splendor of these national treasures. Reflect on the power, authority, and legends that surround these bejeweled symbols of the monarchy. Allow their presence to ignite your imagination and connect you to the rich heritage they represent.

As you wander through the Tower's courtyards and gaze upon its majestic architecture, let your senses be heightened by the atmosphere charged with centuries of history and the tantalizing possibility of encountering the supernatural. Be open to the whispers of the unseen, the chill that races down your spine, and the inexplicable sensations that may accompany your visit.

It is in these moments that you become a part of the Tower's living history, an explorer of the past, and a witness to its enduring allure. Whether you believe in the spectral residents or approach the supernatural with skepticism, the Tower of London offers an experience like no other.

So, answer the call of the Tower. Visit this historic landmark, immerse yourself in its rich tapestry of history, and let its supernatural allure weave its spell upon you. Allow the legends, stories, and mysteries to unfold before your eyes. Form your own impressions, draw your own conclusions, and create memories that will linger long after your visit.

The Tower of London awaits, ready to share its haunted past, its secrets, and its undeniable magnetism. Embrace the invitation, step through its gates, and embark on a journey that will captivate your imagination, enrich your understanding of history, and leave an indelible mark on your soul.

The Tower of London beckons you... will you answer its call?

THE TOWER OF LONDON: THE HAUNTED PAST AND SECRETS OF ROYAL GHOSTS

Sign up to my free newsletter to get updates on new releases, FREE teaser chapters to upcoming releases and FREE digital short stories.

Or visit https://tinyurl.com/olanc

I never spam and you can unsubscribe at any time.

Don't miss out!

Visit the website below and you can sign up to receive emails whenever Oliver Lancaster publishes a new book. There's no charge and no obligation.

https://books2read.com/r/B-A-UNEZ-VYRLC

BOOKS 2 READ

Connecting independent readers to independent writers.

Also by Oliver Lancaster

Chernobyl: Unveiling the tragedy. A Comprehensive Account of the Nuclear Disaster

The Bhopal Gas Tragedy: Unraveling the Catastrophe of 1984

The Deepwater Horizon Oil Spill of 2010: A Disaster Unveiled

Fukushima Fallout: Unveiling the Truth behind the 2011 Nuclear Disaster

Minamata Disease: Poisoned Waters and the Battle for Justice (1932-1968)

Evil Women: Unmasking History's Most Notorious Women

Bundy The Dark Chronicles: America's Infamous Serial Killer

Dahmer The Dark Chronicles: America's Infamous Milwaukee Cannibal

Zodiac The Dark Chronicles: America's Infamous Cryptic Killer

Bigfoot: The Comprehensive Investigation into the Elusive Legend

Chasing Legends: The Truth behind the Chupacabra

Chasing Legends: The Truth behind the Loch Ness Monster

Aokigahara Forest: The Heartbreaking Secrets of Japan's Suicide Forest

The Amityville House: The Haunting Secrets of America's Most Infamous Residence

The Tower of London: The Haunted Past and Secrets of Royal Ghosts
The Winchester Mystery House: The Riddle of Sarah Winchester's Mansion

Watch for more at https://tinyurl.com/olanc.

About the Author

Oliver Lancaster possesses an enchanting charm that effortlessly draws readers into the depths of his literary world. With an insatiable curiosity for the unexplained, he skillfully weaves tales of crime, conspiracy, mystery and the unknown, leaving readers on the edge of their seats.

Nestled away in the seclusion of his garden shed, Oliver finds solace and inspiration in the tranquility of nature. Surrounded by greenery and fragrant blooms, he dives into a realm of imagination, unearthing secrets that lie hidden within his mind.

Accompanying Oliver on his literary ventures is his faithful ginger cat named Italics. With his mesmerizing gaze and mysterious mannerisms, Italics adds an air of intrigue to Oliver's writing process, often curling up on a cushioned chair nearby, watching as words flow effortlessly from his human companion's pen.

When not engrossed in his craft, Oliver indulges in the gentle warmth of his garden with a glass of red wine.

Prepare to be spellbound as you delve into the pages of Oliver Lancaster's novels, for he is a master of the eerie, a weaver of secrets, and an unrivaled guide through the labyrinthine corridors of the human psyche.

Sign up to a free newsletter to get updates on new releases, FREE teaser chapters to upcoming releases and FREE digital short stories.

Read more at https://tinyurl.com/olanc.

Printed in the USA
CPSIA information can be obtained
at www.ICGtesting.com
CBHW070914250524
9098CB00034B/549